American Language Hub

LEVEL 2B
Student's Book
+ access to Student's App

DANIEL BRAYSHAW
JON HIRD

macmillan education

Contents

Irregular Verbs

Base form	Simple past	Past participle
be	was/were	been
become	became	become
begin	began	begun
break	broke	broken
bring	brought	brought
build	built	built
buy	bought	bought
can	could	(been able to)
catch	caught	caught
choose	chose	chosen
come	came	come
cost	cost	cost
cut	cut	cut
drink	drank	drunk
eat	ate	eaten
fall	fell	fallen
feel	felt	felt
find	found	found
forget	forgot	forgotten
get	got	got
give	gave	given
go	went	gone / been
grow	grew	grown
have	had	had
hear	heard	heard
hit	hit	hit
hold	held	held
hurt	hurt	hurt
keep	kept	kept
know	knew	known
leave	left	left
lend	lent	lent
let	let	let
lose	lost	lost
make	made	made
mean	meant	meant
meet	met	met
must	had to	(had to)
pay	paid	paid
put	put	put
read	read	read
ride	rode	ridden
run	ran	run
say	said	said
see	saw	seen
sell	sold	sold
send	sent	sent
set	set	set
shut	shut	shut
sing	sang	sung
sit	sat	sat
sleep	slept	slept
speak	spoke	spoken
spell	spelled	spelled
spend	spent	spent
stand	stood	stood
steal	stole	stolen
take	took	taken
teach	taught	taught
tell	told	told
think	thought	thought
throw	threw	thrown
understand	understood	understood
wear	wore	worn
win	won	won
write	wrote	written

PHONETIC SYMBOLS											
Single vowels			Diphthongs			Consonants					
/ɪ/	fish	/fɪʃ/	/uw/	new	/nuw/	/p/	pen	/pen/	/s/	snake	/sneɪk/
/iː/	bean	/biːn/	/eɪ/	face	/feɪs/	/b/	bag	/bæg/	/z/	zoo	/zuː/
/ʊ/	foot	/fʊt/	/ɔɪ/	boy	/bɔɪ/	/t/	tea	/tiː/	/ʃ/	shop	/ʃɒp/
/uː/	shoe	/ʃuː/	/oʊ/	nose	/noʊz/	/d/	dog	/dɒg/	/ʒ/	television	/'telɪvɪʒən/
/e/	egg	/eg/	/ju/	use	/juz/	/ʧ/	chip	/ʧɪp/	/m/	map	/mæp/
/ə/	mother	/'mʌðər/	/aɪ/	eye	/aɪ/	/ʤ/	jazz	/ʤæz/	/n/	name	/neɪm/
/ɜː/	word	/wɜːrd/	/aʊ/	mouth	/maʊθ/	/k/	cake	/keɪk/	/ŋ/	ring	/rɪŋ/
/ɔː/	talk	/tɔːk/				/g/	girl	/gɜːrl/	/h/	house	/haʊs/
/æ/	back	/bæk/				/f/	film	/fɪlm/	/l/	leg	/leg/
/ʌ/	bus	/bʌs/				/v/	verb	/vɜːrb/	/r/	road	/roʊd/
/ɑː/	arm	/ɑːrm/				/θ/	thing	/θɪŋ/	/w/	want	/wɒnt/
/ɒ/	top	/tɒp/				/ð/	these	/ðiːz/	/j/	yes	/jes/

7 MIND

The greatest thing in life is to keep your mind young.

Henry Ford

A little boy tries to solve the Sunday crossword puzzle, Lancashire, United Kingdom.

OBJECTIVES

- discuss what makes you happy
- write an online comment about the effects of the internet
- talk about intelligence and achievements
- describe an object and say what you use it for
- write a survey report

Work with a partner. Discuss the questions.

1 How can people 'stay young'?
2 Look at the picture. Who is helping whom?
3 What do you do to keep your mind healthy?

7.1 Smile

Discuss what makes you happy

G articles **P** /ə/ (schwa) in *a* / *an* **V** feelings

READING

A Work in groups. Discuss the questions.

1 Do you recognize these famous smiles? What do you know about them?
2 'Laugh and the world laughs with you.' What does this saying mean? Do you agree with its message? Do you have a similar saying in your language?
3 How many times a day do you think a person laughs on average?
4 How is laughing good for our health?
5 How do smiling and laughing help social relationships?

B READ FOR GIST Read *A smile a day …* quickly and check your answers to questions 3, 4 and 5.

C READ FOR DETAIL Are the following statements true (T) or false (F)? Correct the false sentences.

1 Happy people are likely to live to an older age. *T / F*
2 Laughing can have a similar effect to working out in the gym. *T / F*
3 Laughing slows our heartbeat and blood flow. *T / F*
4 Laughing can prevent small health problems. *T / F*
5 The production of chemicals in our brain causes laughter. *T / F*
6 Smiling and laughter began in humans to show there was danger. *T / F*

D SPEAK Work in pairs. Discuss the questions.

1 How many times do you think you laugh each day? When did you last laugh? What did you laugh at?
2 What everyday things make you feel good and put you in a positive mood? (For example, good food, music, new clothes)

A *smile* a day …

We all know that a cheerful state of mind makes us happy but it could also help us to live longer.

Laughing out loud, something we do on average 17 times a day, is particularly good for you. Laughter is a short sound which is repeated, on average, five times a second. It is widely believed that laughing 100 times is equal to ten minutes' light exercise in the gym. In addition, a 2005 study by the University of Maryland School of Medicine showed that laughter lowers blood pressure and there is a healthy increase in heart rate and blood flow. This can lead to a healthier heart and also make you less likely to catch colds and other minor illnesses. The research also suggests that people who are happy are likely to live longer. Laughing also produces chemicals in the brain that make us feel pleased and puts us in a positive mood. Smiling and laughing are also important for social relationships. Experts believe that smiling and laughing in humans began as a way to show relief when danger had passed. It helped the mind and body to feel relaxed and therefore showed trust between people. This stopped people from feeling scared of each other and helped people to connect. So the next time you want to connect with someone, why not start with a smile? It will help them to feel at ease and you might even make a new friend!

Glossary

minor (adj) not very important in comparison with things of the same type
relief (n) a relaxed, happy feeling that you get because a bad situation has ended
state of mind (phrase) the way that you are thinking and feeling at the present time
trust (n) a feeling of confidence in someone that shows you believe they are honest, fair and reliable

GRAMMAR
Articles

A WORK IT OUT Look at the sentences from *A smile a day …* Then complete the rules with *a*/*an*, *the* or – (no article).

***The research** also suggests that people who are happy are likely to live longer.*

*Laughter is **a short sound** which is repeated, on average, five times a second.*

*Smiling and laughing are also important for **social relationships**.*

Articles

1 We use ______________ to refer to something indefinite when it is one of many. We usually use it when we refer to something for the first time.

2 We use ______________ to refer to something definite and which we know. This is usually because it has already been mentioned.

3 We use ______________ to refer to a plural or uncountable noun or something in a general sense.

B Go to the **Grammar Hub** on **page VI**.

C PRACTICE There are two mistakes in each question. Correct the mistakes.

1 The smiley face is a famous image all over world. Why do you think an image is so successful and popular?

2 Do you own or have you ever owned anything with smiley face on it, such as the T-shirt? Where else do we see it?

3 Do you use an emojis or icons in your online messaging? Do you have a favorite emoji? Are there the emojis for your country or culture?

D SPEAK Work in pairs. Ask and answer the questions in Exercise C.

PRONUNCIATION
/ə/ (schwa) in *a* / *an*

7.1 **A** Listen and repeat. What do you notice about the pronunciation of *a* and *an*?

1 Have **a** nice day.

2 We had **a** great time.

3 She's **an** old friend.

4 A smile **a** day keeps the doctor away.

B SPEAK Work in pairs. Student A – go to the **Communication Hub** on **page XXIII**. Student B – go to the **Communication Hub** on **page XXV**.

VOCABULARY
Feelings

A WORK IT OUT Look at the sentences from *A smile a day …* Then choose the correct words to complete the sentences (1–3).

*We all know that a **cheerful** state of mind makes us happy ...*

*It helped the mind and body to feel **relaxed** and therefore showed trust between people.*

*This stopped people from feeling **scared** of each other and helped people to connect.*

1 The words in bold are ***adjectives*** / ***nouns***.

2 They describe ***opinions*** / ***feelings and states of mind***.

3 Words like these ***are always positive*** / ***are always negative*** / ***can be positive or negative***.

B Go to the **Vocabulary Hub** on **page XVIII**.

C SPEAK Work in pairs. When was the last time you felt anxious, confused, pleased, relaxed? Tell your partner.

SPEAKING

A Work in pairs. Do a class survey about what everyday things make people happy. Think of three everyday things that make you happy. Write them down and tell your partner about them.

A: I feel happy when I have a cup of tea in the morning. How about you?
B: Me, too, but I prefer coffee. And going for a walk on a sunny day with a clear blue sky makes me feel good.
A: I agree. A nice day makes everyone feel good!

B Go around the class and ask your classmates what three everyday things make them happy. Write down their answers.

A: Getting into bed after a long day.
B: When I find a bargain in the stores.
C: Relaxing with a good book.

C Work in pairs. Compare your findings. What were the most common answers? What were the most interesting or unusual answers? Work with other pairs and share your answers.

Discuss what makes you happy

7.2 The internet and the brain

Write an online comment about the effects of the internet

G – *used to* P – *used to* V – shortened words

READING

A Work in pairs. Discuss the questions.

1 Look at the picture on the opposite page. What are the people doing?
2 How much time do you spend online? Which devices do you use?
3 What do you like or dislike about the internet?

B Match definitions (1–4) with the words in the box.

addicted	attention span	distracted	memory

1 the length of time that you can pay attention to one thing without becoming bored or thinking about something else ________
2 the ability to remember things ________
3 not able to concentrate on something ________
4 enjoying a particular activity very much and spending as much time as you can doing it ________

C **READ FOR MAIN IDEA** Work in pairs. Look at the title of the show and think of three ways the internet could be killing or damaging our brains. Then read the blog and check your answers.

D **READ FOR DETAIL** Read the comments. Match the comments with the person.

Who …

1 doesn't think the internet is a negative thing?
Tom6 / JennyH / Sue123
2 is losing the ability to concentrate on something for long periods?
Tom6 / JennyH / Sue123
3 thinks the internet has many negative effects on people?
Tom6 / JennyH / Sue123
4 can't remember some things as well as in the past?
Tom6 / JennyH / Sue123
5 thinks it's normal to change the way we use our memory?
Tom6 / JennyH / Sue123

E **SPEAK** Work in pairs. What does 'use it or lose it' mean? What other skills could 'use it or lose it' apply to?

Glossary

adapt (v) to change your ideas or behavior so that you can deal with a new situation
approval (n) a positive opinion that you have towards someone or something that you think is good or suitable
impress (v) if someone or something impresses you, you admire them

Did you see …?
The TV blog for the TV lover *by Anna Frese*

Show: *Is the internet killing our brains?*

Did anyone see that TV show last night, *Is the internet killing our brains?* It was really interesting! First, it looked at the human memory in the 21st century and at how the internet is destroying our memory. This is because today most information is instantly available online and we don't need to remember things. And it said that over time, this could have a negative effect on the brain's memory system – a case of use it or lose it. The show then focused on how the human attention span is decreasing. It said that the brain is naturally easily distracted, and on the internet there is a lot of opportunity for this distraction. Evidence suggests that this is negatively affecting our attention spans and our ability to concentrate.

Finally, the show examined how the 'likes' and other positive comments and approval we receive on social media can be addictive. As a result, people are constantly trying to impress, and social network addiction is becoming a serious issue.

What do you think? Add your comments below:

Tom6 I don't agree with all the points. But, as soon as I start using the net, I find myself looking at site after site. It's very addictive. I can spend hours online and I suddenly realize it's dark outside! I didn't use to be like that. I really do think my attention span is decreasing because of the net. However, they used to say the same thing about the radio and TV when they became popular.

JennyH The Greek philosopher Socrates said that writing would destroy memory because we would not have to remember things. However, Einstein believed that remembering facts was not a good use of our brains or our time. He said we had books to do that for us. What's different about the internet? Humans will adapt to it as they have in the past. I don't see a problem.

Sue123 I disagree with JennyH. I read somewhere that more than 70 percent of people don't know important phone numbers. I used to know all my friends' numbers. Now, I don't know any. We rely on our devices and the internet too much. So I do think it's killing our brains, and in a lot of ways, not just our memories.

PRONUNCIATION
used to

A Listen and repeat. What do you notice about the pronunciation of *used to*? 7.2

1 used to
2 I used to play video games.
3 Phones used to be much bigger.

B SPEAK Work in pairs. Practice saying the sentences. Then listen and check your pronunciation. 7.3

1 We used to speak on the phone a lot more.
2 Computers used to be much bigger.
3 I didn't use to go online much.

VOCABULARY
Shortened words

A Look at the words in **bold** in the sentence from *Did you see ...?* They are shortened words. What are the words short for?

But, as soon as I start using the ***net****, I find myself looking at* ***site*** *after* ***site****.*

B Go to the **Vocabulary Hub** on **page XVIII**.

C SPEAK Work in pairs. Discuss the questions.

1 Why do you think we shorten some words?
2 Is it better to use shortened words in an informal or a formal situation?
3 Can you think of any other shortened words in English?

GRAMMAR
used to

A WORK IT OUT Look at the sentences from *Did you see ...?* Find the missing words and complete the sentences. Then choose the correct words to complete the rule.

1 I can spend hours online, and I suddenly realize it's dark outside! I ________________ be like that.
2 However, they ________________ say the same thing about the radio and TV when they became popular.
3 I ________________ know all my friends' numbers. Now, I don't know any.

used to

We use *used to* to talk about past situations that ***do not exist now / continue now***. The negative form is *didn't use to*.

- I used to work in a phone store.
- She used to have long hair.
- I didn't use to like chatting online.

B Go to the **Grammar Hub** on **page VI**.

C PRACTICE Write five sentences that are true for you with *used to* or *didn't use to*. Use the verbs in the box or your own ideas.

be · be able to · buy · drive · eat · go · have · like · listen to · live · play · read · smoke · watch

I used to read comic books a lot when I was younger.
I didn't use to enjoy learning English.

D SPEAK Work in pairs. Discuss your answers to Exercise C.

SPEAKING

A Read *Did you see ...?* again. Comment on the blog or one of the comments.

B Write notes. Include at least one example of *used to* or *didn't use to*.

C Write about 50 words. Read your comment carefully and check for spelling and grammar.

D DISCUSS Work in pairs. Swap your comments and say whether you agree or disagree with your partner then add a further point.

E Display the comments for your classmates to read. Which ideas and opinions are the most common?

Write an online comment about the effects of the internet

7.3 Intelligence

Talk about intelligence and achievements

V phrasal verbs **G** no article (*school, the school*) **P** practicing *the*: /ðiː/ or /ðə/ **S** listening for the order of events

Wolfgang Amadeus Mozart

Pablo Picasso

Venus Williams

William James Sidis

Garry Kasparov

LISTENING

A SPEAK Work in pairs. Look at the pictures. What do you know about these people? What do they all have in common?

B Match the words (1–2) with the correct definitions (a–b).

1 intelligence
2 knowledge

a all the facts that someone knows about a particular subject
b the ability to understand and think about things

7.4 **C LISTEN FOR KEY WORDS** Listen to the podcast about William James Sidis. Check (✓) what the presenter talks about.

1 Sidis's IQ ☐
2 where he was born ☐
3 his grandparents ☐
4 his language skills ☐
5 his college studies ☐
6 his jobs ☐
7 his friends ☐
8 how he died ☐

Glossary

child prodigy (n) a child who is extremely skillful at something that usually only adults can do
in/out of the public eye (phrase) well known or not well known to people in general
IQ = intelligence quotient (n) a number that represents a person's intelligence, based on the results of a particular type of test
turning point (n) a time when an important change takes place in a situation

7.4 **D** Number the events (a–h) in William James Sidis's life in the order they happened (1–8). Use the information in the box to help you. Then listen again and check.

Listening for the order of events

Listen for words and phrases to help you follow the order of events in a story.

- Words and phrases that tell us when something happened:
  when he was nine *by four years old* *at 11*
  at age 16 *in 1898*
- Words and phrases that tell us that something happened before, at the same time or after something else:
  before *before that* *earlier* *previously*
  while *during* *at the same time*
  after *after this* *soon after* *then* *next*
- Words and phrases that tell us that one thing was a consequence of another:
  as a result *therefore*

a He received a prison sentence. ___
b He became interested in politics. ___
c He taught math at Rice University. ___
d He studied math at Harvard University. ___
e He went to Harvard University to study law. ___
f He gave a lecture in math at Harvard University. ___
g He traveled around the US doing different jobs. ___
h He learned seven languages and also invented one. ___

E SPEAK Work in pairs. Discuss the questions.

1 What were the key events and turning points in William James Sidis's life?
2 Sidis didn't go to school, his mother taught him at home. What are the advantages and disadvantages of this?

VOCABULARY
Phrasal verbs

A Look at the phrasal verbs in **bold** from the podcast about William James Sidis. Match the phrasal verbs (1–6) with the correct meanings (a–f).

1 He was born in 1898 and **grew up** in New York.
2 They **brought** him **up** to have 'a love of knowledge'.
3 His mother **gave up** her job and taught him at home.
4 He also **made up** his own language.
5 He **dropped out** of the university before he finished his degree.
6 He had a **falling out** with his parents and lost contact with them.

a invented
b spent his childhood
c stopped doing something
d left something before finishing it
e stopped being friendly because he had had a disagreement with them
f took care of him until he became an adult

B PRACTICE Complete the sentences with the correct form of a phrasal verb from Exercise A. Use each phrasal verb once.

1 Where did you ________________? What is the neighborhood like? Do you still live there?
2 Who ________________ you ________________? Do you have a big family or a small family?
3 Name something you have ________________. When and why did you stop doing it?
4 When you were a child, did you play traditional games or did you ________________ your own games?
5 Do you know anyone who ________________ of school or college? Why didn't they finish?
6 Have you ever had a ________________ with someone? Did you become friends again?

C SPEAK Ask and answer the questions in Exercise B.

GRAMMAR
No article (*school, the school*)

A WORK IT OUT Look at the sentences from the podcast. Then choose the correct words to complete the rules.

No article (*school, the school*)

Sometimes we use an article (*a, the*) with the words *school, college*, and *prison*. But sometimes we use no article.

- *He didn't go to school.*
- *News reporters followed him everywhere at the college.*
- *At 11, he went to college to study math.*
- *He didn't go to prison and instead he spent a year in a hospital.*

1 When we are referring to the *activity* associated with the place (studying / being a student, being a prisoner) we use ***an article / no article***.
2 When we are referring to the *physical* place, we use ***an article / no article***.

B Go to the **Grammar Hub** on **page VI**.

C PRACTICE Choose the correct words to complete the texts.

Most people go to [1]***the college / college*** at age 18 or 19. However, in 1981, at the age of just 12, Ruth Lawrence became the University of Oxford's youngest ever student. She didn't go to [2]***the school / school*** and her father gave up his job to teach her at home. He also accompanied her everywhere at [3]***the college / a college***.

Nelson Mandela was president of South Africa from 1994 to 1999. Before that, he spent 27 years in [4]***the prison / prison*** for crimes against the government. Eighteen years of this was in [5]***the prison / prison*** on Robben Island, which is seven kilometers out in the ocean from Cape Town.

D SPEAK Work in pairs. Close your books. Tell your partner a story from Exercise C.

PRONUNCIATION
Practicing *the*: /ðiː/ or /ðə/

A SPEAK Work in pairs. Practice saying the sentences.

1 Have you ever been to the East Coast of the United States?
2 No, but I've been to the West Coast.

7.5 **B** Listen and compare your pronunciation. What do you notice about the pronunciation of *the* in each sentence? Why is there a difference?

SPEAKING HUB

A You are going to give a short presentation about a child prodigy. Student A – go to the **Communication Hub** on **page XXII**. Student B – go to the **Communication Hub** on **page XXV**.

B PLAN Read the biography and write notes about:

- the person's early life and education
- his/her talents and abilities
- any key moments or turning points in his/her life
- achievements he/she is famous for
- what he/she did later in life

C ORGANIZE Work in groups. Decide who is going to present which topics and practice your presentation. Use words and phrases from the Listening box to help you.

D PRESENT Give your presentation to your classmates.

Talk about intelligence and achievements

Café Hub

7.4 Neena's dinner

F– describe an object and say what you use it for   P– objects

COMPREHENSION

A SPEAK Work in pairs. Look at the picture. Who do you think says the following, Zac (Z), Gaby (G) or Neena (N)? What do you think happens and who cooks Neena's dinner?

1 Gaby, what's wrong? ___
2 And we promised to cook dinner for her tonight. ___
3 And it's 6:30! ___
4 Who's going to cook? ___
5 I can make pizza! ___
6 I can't think of the word in English. ___
7 A knife? ___
8 You used to work at Pizza Roma? ___
9 Yeah, but I ate too much pizza. ___
10 It looks like Pizza Roma! ___

B Watch the video and check your answers to Exercise A. What is *rallador* in English?

FUNCTIONAL LANGUAGE

Describe an object and say what you use it for

A Complete the phrases with the verbs in the box. You need to use two verbs twice.

forgotten   know   made   think   use

Find out the English word for something
Problem
I've [1] __________ the name of it.
I can't [2] __________ of the word in English.
It's *rallador* in Spanish.
Oh, what's it [3] __________ of?
Description
You [4] __________ it to …
It's a thing you [5] __________ to …
It's [6] __________ of metal.
Check understanding
Do you [7] __________ what I mean?

B 01:09–02:43 Watch part of the video again and check your answers to Exercise A.

USEFUL PHRASES

A Match the useful phrases (1–5) with the phrase that comes before or after it (a–e). Then watch the video again and check your answers.

1 Let me think …
2 Who's going to cook?
3 You can be my assistant chef.
4 You know! 'Un rallador'.
5 Neena says she'll be home soon.

a I'm sorry, I don't understand Spanish.
b Oh, no! We have no time!
c Who's going to cook?
d Cool, good plan.
e Me, for sure.

B How do you say these useful phrases in your language?

MILLY

SAM

NEENA

ZAC

GABY

PRONUNCIATION

Objects

7.6 **A** Match the pictures (a–c) with the conversations (1–3). Then listen and repeat the conversations.

a

b

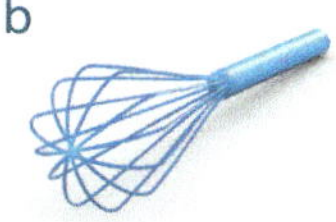

c

1 **A:** What's it made of?
B: It's made of metal. You use it to beat eggs.

2 **A:** What's it made of?
B: It's made of wood. You use it to roll pastry.

3 **A:** What's it made of?
B: It's made of plastic. You use it to wash the dirty dishes.

B SPEAK Work in pairs. Choose another object and write a conversation. Practice saying your conversation.

SPEAKING

1

2

3

4

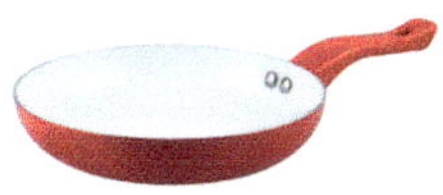

5

6

7

8

Work in pairs. Take turns being Student A and B.

Student A: Look at the pictures and choose an object. Tell your partner:

- the word in your language
- what it's made of
- what you use it for

Student B: Listen and guess the object your partner describes. Tell him/her the number of the object and the name in English.

Describe an object and say what you use it for

➤ Turn to **page XXVI** to learn how to write a survey report.

Unit 7 Review

VOCABULARY

A Choose the best adjective to complete the sentences. Use the information in parentheses to help you.

1 I feel really ***anxious / cheerful*** now that the holidays have started. (*positive*)

2 Lola is a little ***nervous / glad*** about the interview tomorrow. (*negative*)

3 I always feel ***scared / happy*** when I get a lot of 'likes' for my posts on Twitter. (*positive*)

4 I'm really ***nervous / glad*** that you liked the cake I made. (*positive*)

5 Casper didn't go to the top of the building because he was too ***relaxed / scared***. (*negative*)

B Look at the shortened words. Write the missing letters to complete the full words.

1 cell p h o n e

2 info___ ___ ___ ___ ___ ___ ___

3 lab___ ___ ___ ___ ___ ___ ___

4 ___ ___ ___plane

5 ___ ___ ___ ___ ___net

6 mic___ ___ ___ ___ ___ ___ ___

7 ___ ___ ___ ___case

8 ___ ___ ___site

C The phrasal verbs are in the wrong places in the texts. Write them in the correct place. Change the tense if necessary.

I [1]**brought up** in Sheffield. It was just me and my mom, so she [2]**made** me **up** on her own. We had a good relationship, although we argued sometimes and had a [3]**gave up** from time to time. Because I was an only child, I played on my own a lot of the time. This was OK because I had a good imagination and I used to [4]**grew up** my own games. To be honest, I had a really good childhood.

I didn't enjoy college. I found it really difficult. Studying took up all of my time and I had to [5]**drop out** a lot of my hobbies and other activities. I just went to lectures in the day and then studied all evening. So, I decided to [6]**falling out** and get a job instead. It was the best decision I ever made.

GRAMMAR

A Choose the correct article or no article to complete the text.

Humans are not [1]*the / –* only animals that laugh. Other animals such as [2]*the / –* gorillas, chimpanzees and orangutans also laugh. [3]*A / The* main reason for laughter in [4]*the / –* animals is when they are playing. [5]*A / The* laughter indicates that it is [6]*a / the* game and that no one is going to get hurt. [7]*A / –* Laughter has also been observed in [8]*the / –* rats.

B Think about everyday life forty years ago. For each pair of words or phrases, write what we *used to* and *didn't use to* do. Use the verbs in the box.

chat ~~use~~ use watch write and send

1 online maps and GPS / paper maps
We didn't use to use online maps and GPS. We used to use paper maps.

2 on social media / on the phone

3 videos / movies online

4 emails / letters

C Complete the questions about school and college with *a/an*, *the* or – (no article).

SCHOOL AND COLLEGE QUESTIONNAIRE

1 Where did you go to ____ school as a child? Was ____ school close to where you lived?

2 Did you enjoy ____ school? What were your favorite subjects at ____ school?

3 Did you, do you or will you go to ____ college? If so, is ____ college well known for anything?

4 Is there ____ college in the town or city where you grew up? Do most cities in your country have ____ college?

FUNCTIONAL LANGUAGE

Write the missing letters to complete the words. Then match the conversations (1–3) with the pictures (a–c).

1 **A:** What's a protractor?
B: It's a thing you **u**___ ___ to measure and draw angles. It's shaped like half a circle and usually **m**___ ___ ___ of plastic.

2 **A:** I can't **t**___ ___ ___ ___ of the English word for *agrafeuse*. Do you know?
B: Yes, it's stapler, I think.

3 **A:** What's this for?
B: You **u**___ ___ it to draw circles. It's **c**___ ___ ___ ___ ___ a compass.

8 ART

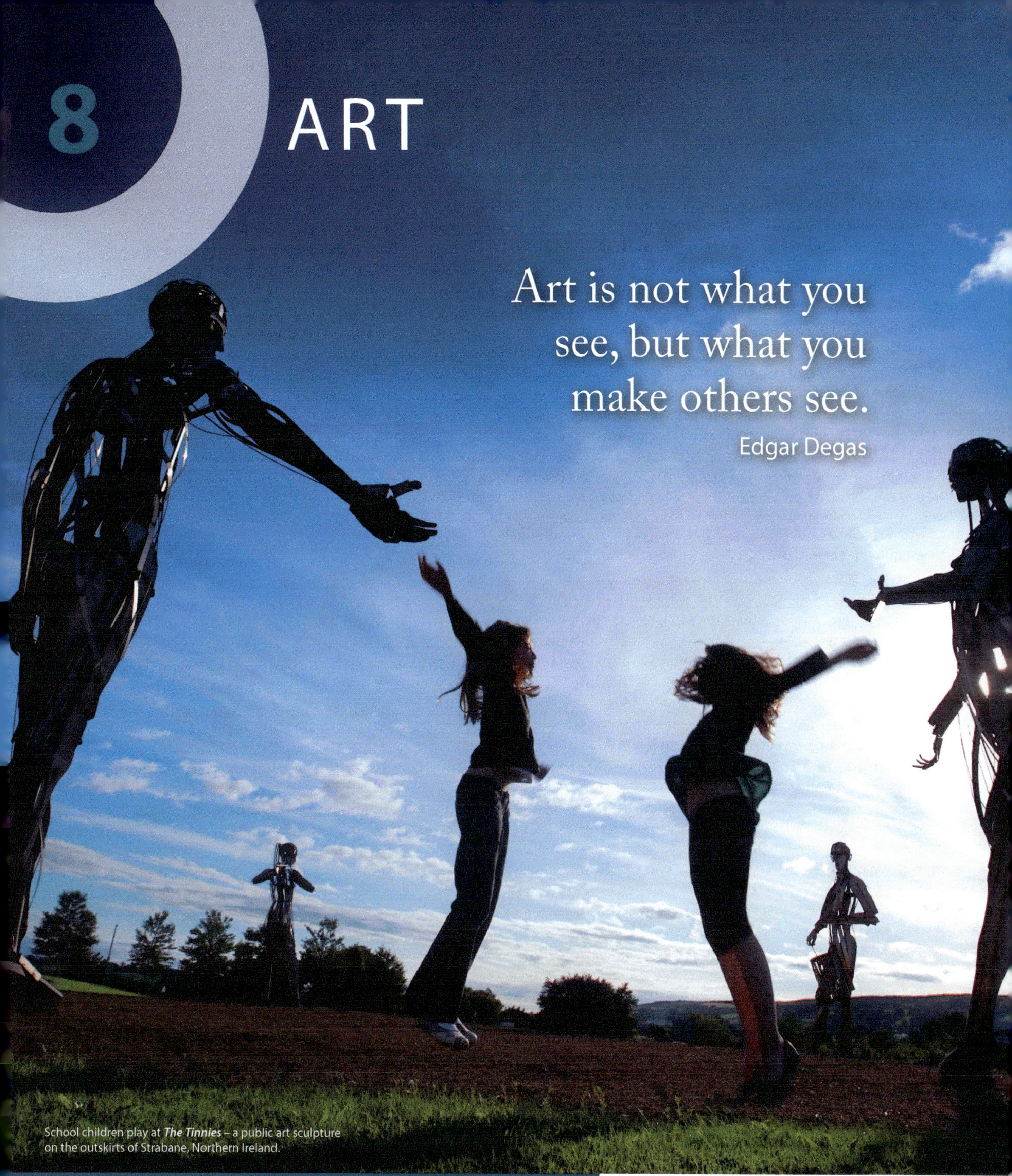

School children play at *The Tinnies* – a public art sculpture on the outskirts of Strabane, Northern Ireland.

OBJECTIVES

- talk about taste in music and your favorite songs
- talk about art and artists
- describe movies and books
- show interest in a topic
- write a review

Work with a partner. Discuss the questions.

1 What different types of art can you name?

2 Look at the picture. Would you like to visit this place?

3 Do you think museums and art galleries should be free? Why/Why not?

8.1 Musical taste

Talk about taste in music and your favorite songs

G reflexive pronouns V music P consonant clusters in words

LISTENING

8.1 **A** Listen to the music extracts (1–7) and match them with the different types of music (a–g).

a rap	___	**e** blues	___
b jazz	___	**f** reggae	___
c rock	___	**g** classical	___
d disco	___		

B SPEAK Work in pairs. Discuss the questions.

1 Can you think of any other types of music?
2 What types of music do you like? What don't you like? Why?
3 Who are your favorite bands or musicians?
4 Why do we like certain types of music? Think of three reasons.

8.2 **C LISTEN FOR MAIN IDEA** Listen to the podcast *Music matters* with Professor Suzy Harrison. What are the three things which explain our taste in music?

Glossary

comforting (adj) making you feel less sad, worried or disappointed
energize (v) to make someone feel excited and enthusiastic
influence (v) to affect the way someone thinks or behaves, also *be influenced by*

8.2 **D LISTEN FOR DETAIL** Choose the correct answer a, b or c, to complete the sentences. Then listen again and check your answers.

1 When we are older, the music from our childhood makes us feel …
  a old.
  b sad.
  c happy.
2 Our first big music influence is generally …
  a our younger brothers and sisters.
  b our older brothers and sisters.
  c our school friends.
3 Music brings people together because we can share …
  a music files and records.
  b our opinions of the music.
  c the mood it creates.
4 We sometimes choose a particular type of music …
  a to create the right conditions for an activity.
  b to give us a break from an activity.
  c to help us forget about an activity.
5 Compared with the past, people today generally like …
  a fewer kinds of music.
  b more kinds of music.
  c the same variety of music.

E SPEAK Work in groups. Discuss the questions.

1 Who has influenced your taste in music, your parents, brothers and sisters, friends or someone or something else?
2 Do you generally like the same kinds of music as your friends? Do you think music is an important part of your friendships?
3 Do you tend to play different kinds of music at different times and when you are in different moods? Give some examples.

GRAMMAR

Reflexive pronouns

8.3 **A** Complete the sentences from the podcast *Music matters* with the pronouns in the box. You need to use one of the pronouns more than once. Then listen and check.

ourselves (x2)   themselves   yourself

1 **We** don't choose this music ________________, of course.
2 So, when **we** start to discover music by ________________, it is influenced by what we listened to when we were growing up.
3 In contrast, for **other people**, musical taste is a way to make ________________ different from other people.
4 And when you're preparing for a night out, **you** might want to energize ________________ and play something loud and full of energy.

B WORK IT OUT Match the sentences in Exercise A (1–4) with the rules (a–c).

Reflexive pronouns

There are several ways we can use reflexive pronouns. The most usual are:

a We use a reflexive pronoun as the object of a verb. This is when the subject and the object are the same person or thing. ___ ___

b We also use a reflexive pronoun after the object of a verb. This is to emphasize the person or thing that does the action. ___

c We use *by* + reflexive pronoun to say we do something alone or with no help. ___

C Go to the **Grammar Hub** on **page VIII**.

D SPEAK Work in pairs. Have you ever …

1 taught yourself to do something (for example, play a musical instrument, play a sport, learn a skill)?
2 designed and/or built something yourself?
3 bought yourself something special?

VOCABULARY

Music

A Go to the **Vocabulary Hub** on **page XIX**.

B Replace the words in **bold** with words in the box with the same or similar meaning.

album band members catchy cover songs gig live lyrics on tour

1 It's a great song. I love the **words**. ______________
2 It's the best **concert** I've been to. ______________
3 They play their own songs and **songs by other bands**. ______________
4 This song is **very easy to remember**. ______________
5 They are **doing a series of concerts** soon. ______________
6 Their first **collection of songs** is their best. ______________
7 I would love to see them **performing a concert**. ______________
8 They have some great **people in the group**, who are excellent musicians. ______________

C SPEAK Work in pairs. Replace the pronouns in Exercise B to make true sentences. Tell your partner.

PRONUNCIATION

Consonant clusters in words

8.4 **A** Underline the consonant clusters in each word. Then listen carefully. Are all the letters in the consonant clusters pronounced?

1 background
2 electric
3 individual
4 influenced
5 keyboards
6 ourselves

8.4 **B** Listen again and repeat the words.

SPEAKING

A Read the text about a radio show. Do you have a similar show in your country?

DESERT ISLAND DISCS

Desert Island Discs is a BBC Radio 4 show in the UK. It was first broadcast in 1942 and since then 3000 episodes have been recorded. Each week, a guest is asked to choose eight songs or other pieces of music they would take if they had to go on a desert island. The guest explains the reasons for their choices.

B Choose three songs or pieces of music to take to a desert island. Which is your number one song?

C Think about how to describe the songs and what you like about them, for example, the lyrics. Write notes about:

- what type(s) of music the songs are
- where the singers or bands are from
- the instruments they play
- what other songs or music the singers or bands are famous for

D Work in pairs. Tell each other what songs you have chosen. Describe the songs and say what you like about them.

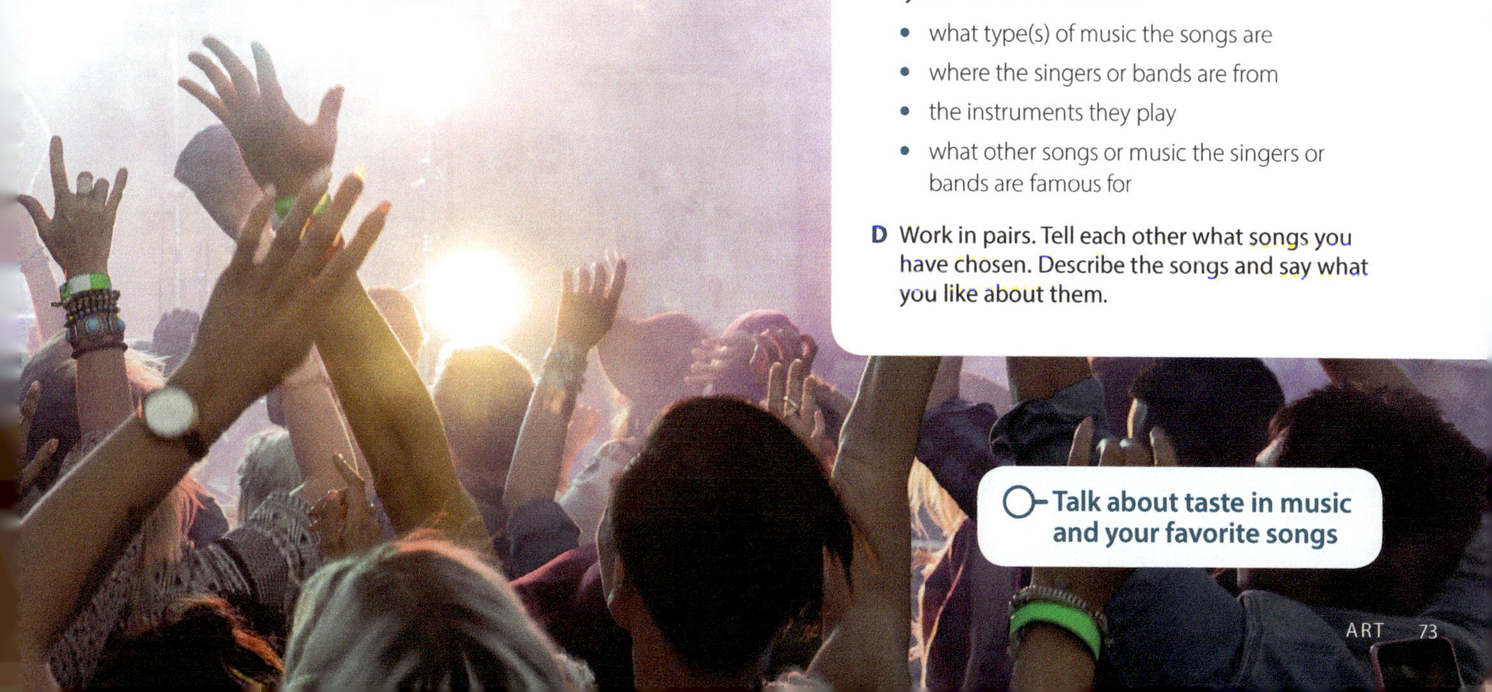

Talk about taste in music and your favorite songs

8.2 Unusual art

Talk about art and artists

V types of art   P /ɪ/ and /iː/   G infinitive of purpose

VOCABULARY
Types of art

A SPEAK Work in pairs. How many artists can you name? What do you know about them or their paintings? Who are the most famous artists from your country?

B Go to the **Vocabulary Hub** on **page XX**.

PRONUNCIATION
/ɪ/ and /iː/

8.5 Listen to the sounds /ɪ/ and /iː/. Then listen and underline the word you hear.

	/ɪ/	/iː/		/ɪ/	/iː/
1	slip	sleep	4	sit	seat
2	ship	sheep	5	pitch	peach
3	live	leave	6	bit	beat

READING

A Work in pairs. Look at the works of art (a–d). What material do you think the artist uses in each one? Tell your partner.

B SCAN Read *Unusual art* quickly and check your answers to Exercise A. Then match the works of art (a–d) with the correct paragraphs (2–5).

C READ FOR DETAIL Read again. Are the following sentences true (T) or false (F)?

1 Anastassia Elias cuts up toilet paper rolls to produce her works of art. T / F

2 Max Zorn uses different colored tape to produce light and dark. T / F

3 Stanislav Aristov uses more than one picture to create his art. T / F

4 Scott Wade mostly creates images of cars and things connected with the automotive industry. T / F

D SPEAK Work in pairs. Which of the works of art do you like best? Why?

UNUSUAL ART

1 Art and artists come in many forms. In this post, we look at four artists who use unusual materials to produce their art.

2 French artist Anastassia Elias uses toilet paper rolls and paper to create everyday scenes of life. She cuts out the image from paper and places it inside the roll. She then illuminates the images from the back, which creates a silhouette.

3 Max Zorn uses brown packing tape to create his works of art. He sticks the tape on glass sheets and illuminates them from the back. He creates dark and light by using thick or thin layers of tape. Originally, he used street lights in Amsterdam in the Netherlands, which is where he is from.

4 Russian artist Stanislav Aristov uses burned matchsticks to create his art. First, he photographs a match after it has finished burning. He then photographs a separate burning flame. Aristov then combines these two images to produce the final picture using picture software. He produces images from nature, such as flowers and animals, as well as everyday objects.

5 Scott Wade creates works of art on the dirty windows of cars. He usually uses artificial dirt to make the car dirty. Wade creates his own images and also recreates famous paintings, such as landscapes and still life. He also produces portraits of famous people. Wade has displayed his work at car shows and other automotive events around the world. He believes that 'dirt is beautiful'.

Glossary

artificial (adj) made by people and used instead of something natural
illuminate (v) to shine a light on something
layer (n) an amount or sheet of a substance that covers a surface
silhouette (n) the dark shape of something

a

b

c

d

1

Little Dancer by Edgar Degas

2

The Scream by Edvard Munch

3

Self-Portrait by Vincent Van Gogh

4

Girl with Balloon by Banksy

GRAMMAR

Infinitive of purpose

A Complete the sentences from *Unusual art*. Write two words in each blank.

1 Max Zorn uses brown packing tape ________________ his works of art.

2 Aristov then combines these two images ________________ the final picture.

3 He usually uses artificial dirt ________________ the car dirty.

B **WORK IT OUT** Look at the sentences in Exercise A and complete the rule. Then find and underline three more examples in the article.

Infinitive of purpose

We use ____________ + ____________ to express the purpose or reason for doing something.

C Go to the **Grammar Hub** on **page VIII**.

D **SPEAK** Complete the sentences with your own ideas to express purpose or reason. Then work in pairs and compare your ideas.

1 I go to museums and galleries …

2 We take pictures …

3 People go on vacation …

SPEAKING

A Look at the pictures above. What do you know about the works of art and the artists (1–4)? Which do you like the best? Why? What other famous works of art do you know?

B Choose one of the works of art or the artist who produced it (1–4) or use your own ideas. Write notes about:

Work of art

- What is the title?
- Who painted or made it? When?
- Is it in a museum or gallery? Where?
- What does it show?
- What materials are used?
- How does it make you feel?
- Have you seen the original?
- Any other information?

Artist

- What is his/her name?
- Where is he/she from?
- When was he/she alive?
- What is his/her style?
- What are his/her famous works of art?
- Do you have a favorite picture by him/her?
- Do you like this artist? Why/Why not?
- Any other information?

C Work in groups. Give your presentation to the group.

Talk about art and artists

Describe movies and books

V movie and book genres; adjectives for describing movies and books P word stress in longer words
G first conditional S identifying contrasts

VOCABULARY

Movie and book genres

A Match the pictures (1–6) with the genres in the box. Then work in pairs to think of movies and books which match the other genres in the box.

> action adventure animated autobiography biography biopic comedy costume drama fairy tale fantasy historical horror musical romantic comedy (rom-com) science fiction (sci-fi) thriller western

1

2

3
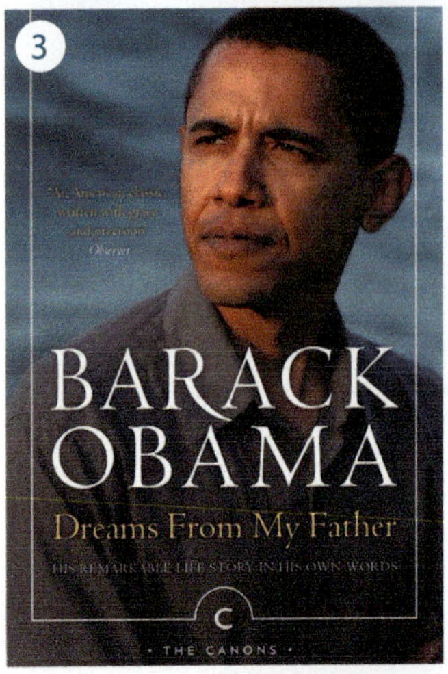

4

5

6

PRONUNCIATION

Word stress in longer words

A Write the movie and book genres in the box in the correct place.

> adventure animated biography comedy fantasy historical musical romantic comedy science fiction

1 •●•	2 ●•••	3 •●••
adventure		

4 ●••	5 •●•●••	6 ●•●•

8.6 **B** Work in pairs. Compare your answers. Then listen and check.

C SPEAK Work in pairs. What genres of movies and books do you enjoy?

LISTENING

A Match the definitions (1–5) with the words in the box.

> engaging gripping memorable sense visualize

1 easy to remember because of being special in some way __________

2 attracting and keeping someone's attention __________

3 to form a picture of something in your mind __________

4 one of the natural abilities most people have to see, hear, smell, taste and feel things __________

5 very exciting and interesting __________

B PREDICT Do you think the following statements refer to movies (M) or books (B)?

1 They allow us to imagine and see things in our own way. __

2 We get to know the characters more. __

3 They connect with our different senses at the same time. __

4 It is an experience we usually share with friends. __

8.7 **C LISTEN FOR GIST** Listen to a podcast comparing movies and books and check your answers to Exercise B.

Glossary

book club (n) a group of people who meet regularly to discuss books
chapter (n) one of the sections into which a book is divided; a chapter usually has a number or a title
character (n) a person in a book or movie
dialogue (n) the words that characters speak in a book or movie

8.7 **D** Match the sentences (1–5) with their contrasting ideas (a–e). Then listen again and check your answers. Use the information in the box to help you.

Identifying contrasts

Listen for linking words and phrases that express a contrast between two ideas:

but, though, however, although	*(but) at the same time*
on the other hand	*compared to*

Listen for phrases that introduce a further contrast:

another (important) difference is	*and one more thing*

1 Books allow the reader to use their imagination.
2 With books, the story generally moves more slowly.
3 We generally watch a movie with other people.
4 Reading is a less sociable activity.
5 People usually say they are disappointed by the movie.

a Book clubs are very popular these days.
b In many cases people actually prefer the movie.
c Reading a book is more individual and personal.
d With a movie the whole story needs to start and finish in 90 minutes.
e With movies we see what the director and the actors want us to see.

8.8 **E LISTEN FOR KEY WORDS** Listen to the extracts. Which linking words or phrases express the contrasting ideas in Exercise D? Make a list.

VOCABULARY

Adjectives for describing movies and books

A Look at the sentences from the podcast. Complete the adjectives with the missing vowels (*a, e, i, o, u*).

1 I think this makes the experience more personal and _e_ng_a_g_i_ng.
2 A movie can be much more ___xc___t___ng and gr___pp___ng than a book.
3 Music can also make the movie more ___nt___r___st___ng and m___m___r___bl___.
4 Compared to the book, people usually say they are d___s___pp___ ___nt___d by the movie.

8.9 **B** Read the information in the box and choose the correct option in the sentences below. Listen and check.

Adjectives for describing movies and books

We use adjectives ending in *-ing* to talk about what caused the feeling.

- *The movie was disappoint**ing**.*

We use adjectives ending in *-ed* to talk about how we feel.

- *I was disappoint**ed**.*

1 It was totally ***engaged / engaging*** and the acting was ***amazed / amazing***.
2 I was, well, a little ***bored / boring*** by the end. It isn't very memorable I'm afraid.
3 You won't be ***disappointed / disappointing***. The singing was incredible.
4 It's really ***gripped / gripping***. And it's very ***moved / moving*** and sad, too.

GRAMMAR

First conditional

A WORK IT OUT Look at the first conditional sentences below. Then choose the correct words to complete the rules.

*If you **want** a great night out, you **should see** this movie.*

*If you **remind** me, **I'll lend** it to you.*

*If you **like** musicals, **you'll love** it.*

First conditional

1 We use the first conditional to talk about ***impossible / possible*** situations in the future.
2 Conditional sentences usually have two clauses: the *if*-clause and the main clause. To make a first conditional sentence, we use:
   - *If* + ***present tense / will*** and ***present tense / will*** + base form.
3 We ***can / can't*** use other modal verbs (for example, *can, could, might, should*) instead of *will* in the main clause.

B Go to the **Grammar Hub** on **page VIII**.

SPEAKING HUB

8.10 **A** Listen to Salli recommending a movie. What does she talk about?

1 the movie type or genre
2 the main story
3 the actors, the director, the writer
4 what she likes about it
5 how it made her feel

B PLAN You are going to recommend a movie or book. Decide which movie or book you are going to talk about and write notes about the topics in Exercise A.

C ORGANIZE Use adjectives for describing movies or books and at least one first conditional sentence (*If you like ..., you'll love ...*).

D DISCUSS Work in groups. Recommend the movie or book you chose to your group.

Describe movies and books

Café Hub

8.4 First date

Ⓕ– show interest in a topic   Ⓟ– intonation

COMPREHENSION

A ▶ **SPEAK** Work in pairs. Which topics do you think Milly and Zac will talk about on their first date? Then watch the video and check your answers.

children culture family food home marriage money music the weather work

B ▶ Are the sentences true (T) or false (F)? Correct the false sentences. Then watch the video again and check your answers.

1 Zac arrives first at the park. T / F
2 Milly knows the band Zac is listening to. T / F
3 Zac and Milly have tickets to the same show. T / F
4 It's Milly's birthday today. T / F
5 Zac loves English food. T / F
6 Milly likes English culture. T / F
7 Zac thinks Milly is shy. T / F
8 Milly wants to go home. T / F

FUNCTIONAL LANGUAGE

Show interest in a topic

A Complete the replies (1–11) with the words in the box.

are believe did do for kidding neither no really so too

Comment	Reply
	Show surprise
[music playing]	1 ________ way! Is this Gold Sounds?
It's their new record.	2 ________ real?
I have tickets to their show.	You're 3 ________! I don't 4 ________ it!
I'm going with my sister.	5 ________ you?
She got the tickets for my birthday.	She 6 ________?
It's today.	7 ________? It's your birthday today?
I like that about you.	You 8 ________?
	Show you understand
I miss my family.	9 ________ do I.
I'm not crazy about English food.	10 ________ am I.
I feel like I can be myself here.	Me, 11 ________.

B ▶ Watch the video again and check your answers.

MILLY

SAM

NEENA

ZAC

GABY

Glossary
Really? **(interjection) (British)** = For real? **(phrase) (American)**
You're joking! **(phrase) (British)** = You're kidding! **(phrase) (American)**

PRONUNCIATION
Intonation

8.11 **A** Listen to the replies from Functional language Exercise A. Write them in the correct place. Then listen again and check your answers.

Rising intonation	Falling intonation
	No way!

8.11 **B** Listen again and repeat the replies. Copy the intonation.

SPEAKING

A Write a short sentence about the following topics:

1. something surprising
   I have tickets for Rihanna!
2. something shocking
   ______
3. something that isn't true
   ______
4. something about the past
   ______
5. something about the future
   ______
6. something you like
   ______
7. something you don't like
   ______

B Work in pairs. Take turns. Student A – read out your sentences. Student B – show interest and reply.

Show interest in a topic

➤ Turn to **page XXVII** to learn how to write a review.

Unit 8 Review

VOCABULARY

A Rearrange the letters of the words in **bold**. The first and last letters are in the correct place.

1 Do you listen to whole **ablmus** or do you usually listen to individual songs?

2 Do you pay much attention to the **lriycs** of a song or do you mostly listen to the music?

3 Do you have a favorite **sigenr** or musician (**giuristat**, **dmruemr**)?

4 Do you go to many **ggis**? What was the last band you saw **lvie**? Was there a good **lhgit sohw**? Where were you in the **aduenice** – near the **satge** or far away from it?

B Complete the quiz questions with the words in the box. There is one word you do not need. Then take the quiz.

abstract exhibit gallery landscape portrait sculpture still life

ART QUIZ
How much do you know?

1 Which is the world's most visited art ________?
a The British Museum, London
b The Metropolitan Museum of Art, New York
c The Louvre, Paris

2 It toured the world in the 1970s and is the most visited ________ of all time. What was it?
a *The Treasures of Tutankhamun*
b The *Art of the Aztecs*
c *The Visions of Van Gogh*

3 *David* by Michelangelo is perhaps the most famous ________ in the world. How tall is it?
a 5.17 meters
b 7.15 meters
c 1.75 meters

4 *Sunflowers* is one of the world's most famous collections of ________ paintings. Who painted them?
a Leonardo da Vinci
b Vincent van Gogh
c Pablo Picasso

5 *Girl with a Pearl Earring* by Johannes Vermeer is a famous ________ painting. When did Vermeer paint it?
a 1465
b 1665
c 1865

6 Pablo Picasso was most famous for his ________ art. Where was Picasso born?
a France
b Italy
c Spain

C Match the movie and book genres (1–5) with the descriptions (a–e). Then choose the correct adjectives. Which of the descriptions are positive (P) and which are negative (N)?

1 comedy
2 thriller
3 biography
4 fantasy
5 horror

a It isn't scary at all and I was pretty *bored / boring* for most of it.
b It's really funny. Go see it, you won't be *disappointed / disappointing*.
c It has a lot of strange creatures in it. The visuals are *amazed / amazing*.
d The story of his life was very *engaged / engaging* and very *moved / moving*.
e It's very *excited / exciting* and *gripped / gripping*. I couldn't stop reading it.

GRAMMAR

A Complete the conversations with the correct reflexive pronouns.

1 **A:** Great gig! Who's the last song by?
B: We wrote it ________.

2 **A:** I like Jenny's website. Who designed it for her?
B: I think she designed it ________.

3 **A:** Did you have guitar lessons or teach ________?
B: I taught ________.

B Complete the sentences with the best verb to express purpose. Use *to* + infinitive.

1 We're going to the museum ________ the Picasso exhibit.
2 I mostly use my laptop ________ movies.
3 I started a hobby ________ new people.
4 Can I use your phone ________ my friend?

C Complete 1–3 with the correct form of the verbs in parentheses.

1 If you ________ (*see*) Janice this evening, ________ (*you / say*) hello from me?

2 **A:** If we ________ (*miss*) the bus, we ________ (*get*) a taxi.
B: OK, or if it ________ (*stop*) raining, we ________ (*walk*). It isn't far to the movie theater.

3 If you ________ (*like*) reggae, you ________ (*love*) this band. I ________ (*get*) you a ticket if you ________ (*like*).

FUNCTIONAL LANGUAGE

A Complete the conversations with the words in the box.

believe did do real so too

1 **A:** Alice got a place in the art course.
B: She ________? That's great news.

2 **A:** Jimmy's band has a record contract.
B: For ________?

3 **A:** Did you know that the movie won three Oscars?
B: Really? I don't ________ it! It was terrible.

4 **A:** I'm going see Jake's new band tonight.
B: Yeah. Me, ________.

5 **A:** I want to go to the Damien Hirst exhibit.
B: You ________? I didn't think you liked his stuff.

6 **A:** I love musicals.
B: ________ do I!

9 MONEY

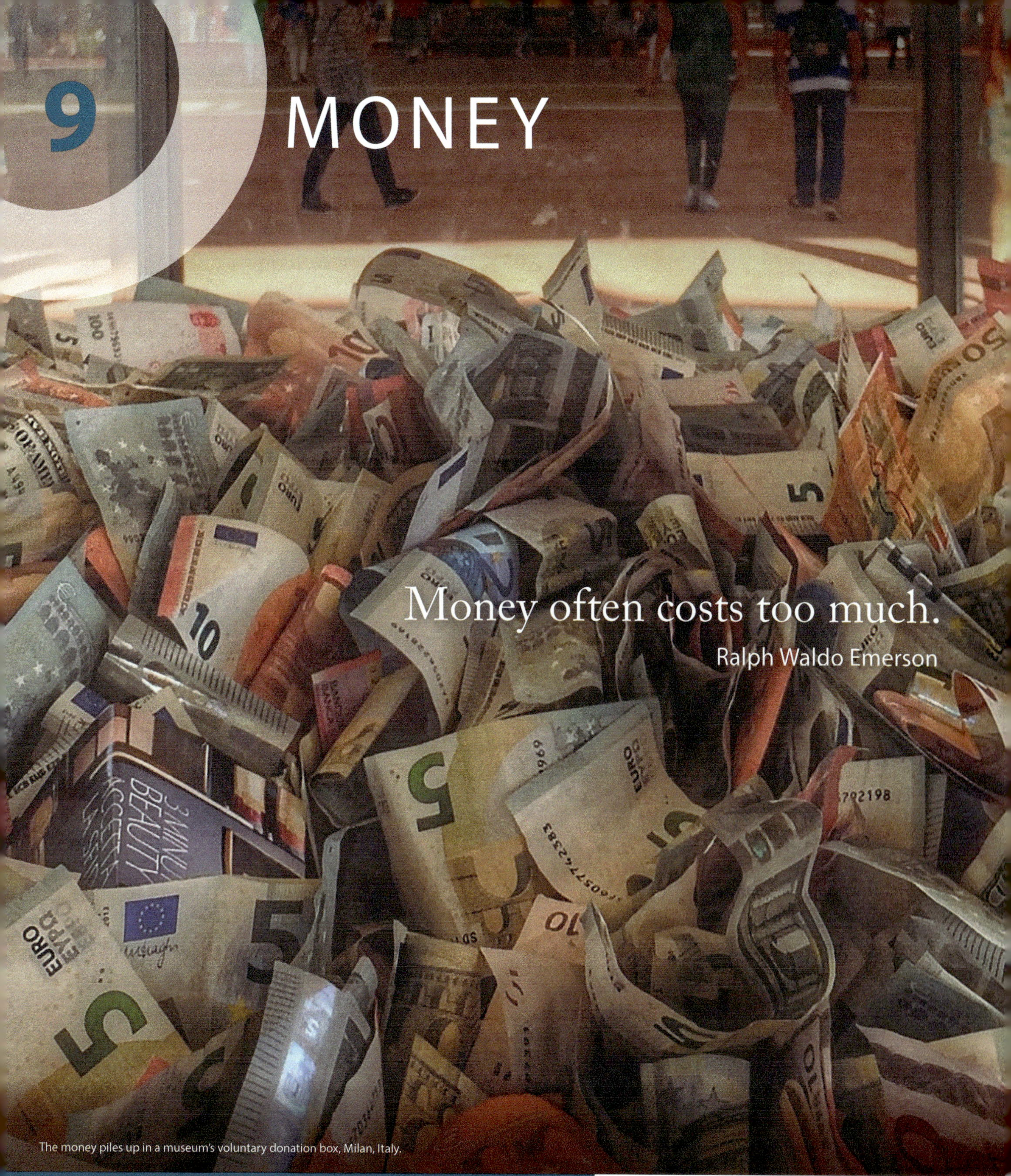

The money piles up in a museum's voluntary donation box, Milan, Italy.

OBJECTIVES

- talk about attitudes toward money and about spending money
- talk about philanthropy and charities
- discuss your skills and how they could help others
- go shopping for clothes and ask for a refund
- write a 'for sale' advertisement

Work with a partner. Discuss the questions.

1 Is money important?
2 Read the quote. What do you think Emerson meant? Do you agree?
3 Do you spend money every day? What do you buy?

9.1 Spending money

Talk about attitudes toward money and about spending money

P /ɑː/, /ʌ/ and /æ/ G second conditional V prepositions in money phrases

READING

A Match the words (1–4) with the definitions (a–d).

1 obsessed	a something that you own
2 gain	b to get something
3 inspire	c to give someone the enthusiasm to do something
4 possession	d considering something so important that you are always thinking about it

B READ FOR MAIN IDEA Read *How to buy happiness*. Write the paragraph headings in the correct place. There is one heading you do not need.

- **a** Try something new
- **b** Discover yourself
- **c** Take your time
- **d** Open your mind

C READ FOR DETAIL Read again and answer the questions.

1. Which makes us feel better for longer, possessions or experiences?
2. In what three ways does Julie benefit from traveling?
3. What does Carmen learn from meeting people?
4. According to Carmen, how can traveling improve our character?
5. What does Hugo think can make us lazy?
6. Why does Hugo think experiences inspire us to do more?

D SPEAK Work in pairs. Discuss the questions.

1. Do you agree with the article? Why/Why not?
2. Have you spent money on experiences such as travel? What did you do? Were the experiences positive or negative? Why?

HOW TO BUY HAPPINESS

We live in a society that is obsessed with spending money – a society that is obsessed with materialism. When we buy things, it gives us happiness. But this feeling usually lasts only for a short time. Experiences, on the other hand, stay with us for a long time after they have finished. Therefore, if we spent more of our money on experiences, we would gain something that can last a lifetime. Here are three more reasons we should spend more time and money on experiences and three people who agree with this advice.

1 ______________________________

Julie from the UK believes travel is an important experience. She says, 'Traveling helps us to discover our interests. I'm always saving up so I can go away at least once or twice a year. It helps me to discover what I like and what I don't like. It helps me to understand who I am. I think we wouldn't find out these things if we didn't spend money on experiences.'

2 ______________________________

Carmen from Italy also believes that travel is important. She says, 'I spend a lot of my money on traveling. It helps us to see different points of view. As you travel, you meet new people with different ideas and opinions to your own. This teaches us some important life lessons and helps us to understand the world.' Carmen also believes that traveling helps you to become more independent and more confident.

Glossary

materialism (n) the belief that money and possessions are the most important aspects of human existence

3 ______________________________

According to Hugo from Brazil, our experiences can inspire us. He says, 'It's always good to do something that is new. If we didn't do anything different, we might become lazy. We don't have to climb Mount Everest, but we can do things like learn to play a musical instrument, start a new sport or simply do something new for the first time. This will make us feel good and give us a sense of achievement. This will then inspire us to try more things in life. So, my attitude toward money is to spend it on experiences as much as possible!'

So, before you buy your next possession, ask yourself 'Is there an experience I can spend my money on instead?' This could be a night out with friends, a concert or a sporting event, or maybe a weekend away or a vacation. Whatever we choose, it will make us rich with memories and life lessons.

PRONUNCIATION

/ɑː/, /ʌ/ and /æ/

A Look at the underlined letters in each word. What sound do they make? Write the words in the correct place.

after discover happiness last
money much ~~past~~ travel up

/ɑː/	/ʌ/	/æ/
past		

B Listen and check. Then listen again and repeat the words.

9.1

C SPEAK Work in pairs. Practice saying the sentences. Listen to your partner and check their pronunciation.

1 Happiness usually lasts only for a short time.
2 Traveling helps us to discover our interests.
3 Is there an experience I can spend my money on instead?

GRAMMAR

Second conditional

A WORK IT OUT Look at the second conditional sentences from *How to buy happiness*. Write the missing words. Then choose the correct words to complete the rules.

1 If we ________________ more of our money on experiences, we ________________ something that can last a lifetime.
2 We ________________ these things if we ________________ money on experiences.
3 If we ________________ anything different, we ________________ lazy.

Second conditional

1 We use the second conditional to talk about ***real / unreal or impossible*** situations in the present or future.
2 Conditional sentences usually have two clauses: the *if*-clause and the main clause. To make a second conditional sentence, we use:
- *If* + ***simple past / would*** and ***simple past / would*** + *base form*.

3 We ***can / can't*** use other modal verbs (for example, *can, could, might, should*) instead of *would* in the main clause.

B Go to the **Grammar Hub** on **page X**.

VOCABULARY

Prepositions in money phrases

A Complete the sentences with the correct prepositions. Then read *How to buy happiness* again and check your answers.

1 I'm always saving ________ so I can go away at least once or twice a year.
2 I spend a lot of my money ________ traveling.
3 My attitude ________ money is to spend it on experiences as much as possible.

B Complete the sentences with the prepositions in the box.

by for from in out out of to

1 I usually take money ________ the ATM once or twice a week. I take ________ 20 or 30 dollars each time.
2 For things under, say, five dollars, I generally pay ________ cash. I usually pay ________ things over five dollars ________ card.
3 I occasionally borrow money ________ my friends and I also sometimes lend it ________ them. But it's never usually more than 10 or 20 dollars.

C SPEAK Work in pairs. Change the sentences in Exercises A and B so they are true for you. Ask your partner questions to find out more information.

A: I'm always saving up so I can go to concerts and music festivals.

B: My attitude toward money is spend a little and save a little.

SPEAKING

A Work in groups. Think about different situations and make choices. Group A – go to the **Communication Hub** on **page XXII**. Group B – go to the **Communication Hub** on **page XXV**.

B Work in pairs. Ask your partner your new questions and make a note of their answers.

C Work in groups. Compare your findings. How similar or different are they? What are the most common or unusual answers?

Talk about attitudes toward money and about spending money

9.2 Getting and giving

Talk about philanthropy and charities

V verbs connected with money **P** /s/ and /z/ **G** essential adjective clauses

VOCABULARY

Verbs connected with money

A Complete the facts below with the correct form of the verbs in the box.

donate ~~earn~~ give away lose make owe raise support

MONEY facts

1. In 1979, baseball player Nolan Ryan became the first professional athlete to ___earn___ $1 million a year.
2. Microsoft's Bill Gates, businessman Warren Buffet and Facebook's Mark Zuckerberg have all said they will ______ 95 percent of their money to charity. A number of other philanthropists have also made the same promise.
3. Spanish actress Penélope Cruz ______ many charities (organizations that give money and help to people who need it). In fact, she gave all of her salary from her first Hollywood movie to charity.
4. On September 16, 1992, Hungarian-born businessman George Soros ______ $1 billion. This is the biggest single-day profit in history.
5. Eike Batista was once Brazil's richest person with $30 billion. However, unfortunately he ______ it all. In fact, in 2014, he ______ $30 billion to the banks.
6. The London Marathon ______ more money for charity than any other sports event. In 2016, this was almost £60 million.
7. Philanthropy is about giving money to people who need it. Philanthropists across the world ______ around $500 billion a year to charity and other organizations. The main givers include the United States, China, United Kingdom, Russia, Australia and Switzerland.

B Complete the questions with the correct verbs. Use the *Money facts* to help you.

1. Have you ever **d**______ money to a charity? If so, what does the charity **r**______ money for?
2. If you could give a lot of money to charity, which charities or organizations would you **s**______? Why?
3. Do you agree that all people who **e**______ a lot of money or who have **m**______ a lot of money should **g**______ some of it **a**______ to charities? Why/Why not?

C **SPEAK** Ask and answer the questions in Exercise B.

PRONUNCIATION

/s/ and /z/

A **SPEAK** Work in pairs. Look at the words in the box. Do the letters in **bold** make a /s/ or a /z/ sound? Underline the /s/ sounds and circle the /z/ sounds.

across also baseball Facebook givers promise raises salary same supports Switzerland visit

B Listen and check. Then listen again and repeat the words.

9.2

LISTENING

A Work in pairs. Discuss the questions.

1. What you know about the people in the pictures? What do you think they have in common?
2. Which other philanthropists do you know?

Andrew Carnegie

John D. Rockefeller

Bill Gates, Melinda Gates, Warren Buffet

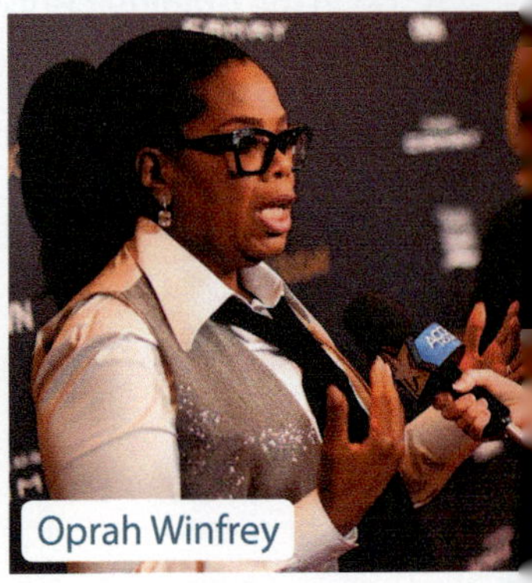

Oprah Winfrey

B LISTEN FOR KEY WORDS Listen to Part 1 of a lecture about philanthropists. Complete the first column with the people in the pictures on page 84.

9.3

Names of philanthropists	Numbers	What the numbers mean
John D. Rockefeller	$540m, 1937	*John D. Rockefeller gave away about $540 million. He died in 1937.*
	$350m, 90 percent	
	half a billion dollars	
	tens of billions of dollars, 2010	

C LISTEN FOR KEY INFORMATION Listen again. What do the numbers mean? Write your answers in the third column in Exercise B.

9.3

D LISTEN FOR GIST Listen to Part 2 of the lecture. Which is the best explanation of the Giving Pledge? Choose a, b or c.

9.4

The Giving Pledge asks people to give at least 50 percent of their wealth to charity …

a when they die.

b before they die.

c in the next ten years.

E LISTEN FOR MAIN IDEA Listen again. Check (✓) the names of the philanthropists who have joined the Giving Pledge. Put an ✗ in the box for the ones who have not.

9.4

1 Mark Zuckerberg ☐
2 Richard Branson ☐
3 Ann Gloag ☐
4 Carlos Slim ☐
5 Sara Blakely ☐
6 Li Ka-shing ☐
7 Meg Whitman ☐
8 Azim Premji ☐

F LISTEN FOR DETAIL Listen again. Write the names of the philanthropists.

9.4

1 *Azim Premji* has set up a university.

2 ________ has given away one quarter of his or her wealth.

3 ________ would refuse to join the Giving Pledge if he or she was invited.

4 ________ believes that there should be more women in powerful positions.

5 ________ believes the best way to end poverty is through education and jobs.

6 ________ is mostly concerned with education and health in his or her own country.

GRAMMAR

Essential adjective clauses

A WORK IT OUT Underline the adjective clauses in the sentences from the lecture. Then complete the rules with *who, which* or *that*.

1 And today, there are many celebrities who have given money to charity.

2 Let's now look at five modern-day philanthropists that you may or may not have heard of.

3 Instead she has her own charity that focuses on the environment and education.

4 He has also set up a university which promotes educational thinking.

Essential adjective clauses

1 An essential adjective clause gives information about and identifies a noun (a person or thing). It comes after the noun and starts with a relative pronoun.

We use [a] ________ when the noun is a person.

We use [b] ________ when the noun is a thing.

We can use [c] ________ for a person or a thing.

2 We can leave out the relative pronoun when the word following the noun is a subject (*I, you, people, the charity*).

- *Let's now look at five modern-day philanthropists ~~that~~ you may or may not have heard of.*

B Go to the **Grammar Hub** on **page X**.

C You are going to write some definitions. Student A – go to **page XXII**. Student B – go to **page XXIV**.

D SPEAK Complete the sentences with the correct relative pronouns and your own ideas. Leave out the relative pronoun if possible. Then, work in groups and share your ideas.

1 A famous person ________ I admire is …

A famous person I admire is Michelle Obama.

2 A charity ________ does a lot of good is …

3 Someone ________ has influenced me a lot is …

4 A global issue ________ I think is important is …

5 A person ________ has positively influenced society is …

SPEAKING

A Work in groups and discuss the questions.

1 Which charities do you know?

2 What do you know about them?

3 Why do people give to charity?

4 Do you think it is better to give time or money? Why?

Talk about philanthropy and charities

9.3 Who needs money?

Discuss your skills and how they could help others

G gerunds V *make* and *do* expressions P /ʒ/ and /dʒ/ S using context to guess unknown words

READING

A Did you exchange anything with other people when you were younger, for example, toys, books or soccer cards? What about later in life?

B **PREDICT** Look at the title of the article and at the glossary. What do you think the article is about?

C **SCAN** Read *Bartering is back* and complete the notes.

1 Kyle McDonald started a website, and after one year exchanged a ______________ for a ______________.

2 Websites such as Craigslist.org: People can exchange ______________ with each other.

3 Antonio Puri exchanged a ______________ for ______________.

4 Time banks: For every ______________ you work, you earn ______________.

5 Basic rule: Ask a ______________ for what you are offering. Need to agree what is ______________.

BARTERING IS BACK

Back in 2005, Canadian Kyle MacDonald was making a living delivering pizzas, but he dreamed of owning his own house. So, one day he set up a website and offered a red paper clip in exchange for 'something bigger and better'. One year later, and after 14 exchanges, he had swapped the paper clip for a house! First, he swapped the paper clip for a pen. After that, the trades included a snowmobile, a van, an afternoon with rock star Alice Cooper and a role in a Hollywood movie. Finally, he swapped the movie role for a house.

But trading or bartering one item for another is nothing new. It was how people 'shopped' before the invention of money. And today, bartering is back. The number of people who use websites such as Craigslist.org, where you can exchange one item or service for another, is increasing. Some websites, such as babysitterexchange.com, provide just one service, while other sites cover a range of items and services. People have exchanged yoga lessons and language lessons for decorating, offered dog-walking and rides to the airport in exchange for theater and concert tickets, and some people will offer to do your shopping, cleaning or ironing in exchange for items they need. People also offer to trade professional services such as legal advice and accountancy. Antonio Puri, an artist based in Philadelphia in the US, was in his dentist's chair when he noticed there were no paintings on the walls. He told his dentist 'You need art. How about doing a trade?' Puri made him an offer and swapped a $1200 painting for his dental treatment.

Time banks are another recent development. You register at your local *Time Bank*'s website and list the services you have to offer or like doing. For each hour of work you provide to another member, you earn a certain number of 'time credits'. You can then spend your 'time credits' on another service on the site that someone else enjoys doing.

Doing your research and suggesting realistic prices are the basic rules with both barter sites and time banks. It's important not to try to make a profit. At the same time, if someone does you a favor, don't give them something below its value. If you do this, the system will break down and stop working. If you are bartering, it is important to agree with the other person what is a fair exchange. So, for example, you might agree that a driving lesson is equal to two haircuts or that fixing someone's washing machine is equal to a half-hour guitar lesson.

So, next time you need something, don't reach for your wallet or bankcard. Who needs money when you can trade?

Glossary

barter (v) to exchange goods or services for other goods or services instead of using money

D Do you know the meaning of the words and phrases in the box? Find them in the text and use the information in the box to work out or check their meaning.

break down   dental   favor   making a living   set up   swapped   treatment

Using context to guess unknown words

If there is a word or phrase in a text that you don't know or understand, try to guess the meaning from context. Read the sentence before and the sentence after to help you.

Think about the wider context, for example, the topic and message of the paragraph.

Identify the word's grammatical form and function to help give it meaning.

If you can't work out the meaning, keep reading. You may read something later which helps you to understand the word.

E Guess the meaning of the words in **bold** (1–3). Then match them with their definitions (a–c).

Bartering is about communities. It connects people. It [1]**fosters** human contact. For something [2]**tangible**, like a couch or a bike, it is easy to decide a price. But to work out a price for a service is more [3]**tricky**.

a difficult to do

b helps something to develop over a period of time

c something that you can touch

F **SPEAK** Work in groups. Do you think bartering items and services is a good idea? What are the pros and the cons?

GRAMMAR
Gerunds

A Look at the gerunds in **bold** in the phrases from *Bartering is back*. Then choose the correct words to complete the rules.

... but he dreamed of ***owning*** *his own house.*

... that someone else enjoys ***doing****.*

Doing *your research and suggesting realistic prices are the basic rules ...*

... the system will break down and stop ***working****.*

Gerunds

1 Gerunds are types of *nouns / verbs*.
2 We use gerunds *after / before* prepositions.
3 We can use gerunds directly after *some / all* verbs.
4 We can use gerunds as *subjects only / objects only / subjects or objects*.

B Go to the **Grammar Hub** on **page X**.

C **SPEAK** Work in pairs. Discuss the questions.

- What are you looking forward to doing this weekend?
- What do you like/dislike spending your money on?
- Are you good at saving money? Why/Why not?

VOCABULARY
make and *do* expressions

A Complete the sentences from *Bartering is back* with the correct form of *make* or *do*. Then check your answers in the article.

1 Back in 2005, Canadian Kyle MacDonald was ___making___ **a living** delivering pizzas.
2 Some people will offer to ________ your **shopping, cleaning** or **ironing** in exchange for items they need.
3 Puri ________ him **an offer** and swapped a $1200 painting for his dental treatment.
4 ________ your **research** and suggesting realistic prices are the basic rules with both barter sites and time banks.
5 It's important not to try to ________ **a profit**. At the same time, if someone ________ you **a favor**, don't give them something below its value.

B Go to the **Vocabulary Hub** on **page XX**.

PRONUNCIATION
/ʒ/ and /dʒ/

9.5 **A** Listen to the sounds /ʒ/ and /dʒ/. They are very similar. Then listen and say whether you hear the sound /ʒ/ or /dʒ/ in each word.

1 exchange   3 decision   5 suggest
2 language   4 Asia

9.6 **B** Listen, check and repeat the words.

SPEAKING HUB

A You are going to swap skills and services with your classmates. Follow the instructions.

- Think about two or three skills and services that you can offer (music, language or driving lessons; help with cleaning, gardening; accounting advice).
- Decide on the price of your service. For example, a one-hour driving lesson = $30, or an hour's ironing = $10.

B **SPEAK** Walk around the class and find out what skills and services your classmates are offering and how much they cost.

C **PLAN** When you have spoken to at least five people, decide which three skills and services you would like.

D **DISCUSS** Try to exchange skills or services with your classmates. For example, you could offer a one-hour driving lesson in exchange for three hours of ironing.

Discuss your skills and how they could help others

Café Hub

9.4 Difficult customer

F– go shopping for clothes and ask for a refund
P– adding emphasis

COMPREHENSION

A SPEAK Work in pairs. Think of a time when you bought something in a clothing store (or any store) and then returned it. Discuss the questions.

1 What was the item?
2 What was the problem?
3 What happened in the end?

B ▶ Watch the video and answer the questions in Exercise A.

C How would you describe Milly? How would you describe the customer? Choose adjectives from the box or use your own ideas.

anxious dishonest friendly kind relaxed scared shy

FUNCTIONAL LANGUAGE

Go shopping for clothes and ask for a refund

A Work in pairs. Change the highlighted words for more polite words in the box.

Can you enter Here's your refund I'd like a refund I'd like to I'll take it I'm looking for kind of thing would you like

Sales clerk	Customer
Can I help you?	I want [1] __________ a gift for my nephew. He's 15.
What exactly [2] __________ are you looking for?	A blue sweater.
	How much is this sweater?
$15	Great. I want it [3] __________.
How do you want [4] __________ to pay, cash or card?	Card, please.
Put in [5] __________ your pin?	
Would you like me to gift wrap it for you?	Yes, please.
OK.	
Two weeks later	
	I want to [6] __________ return this, please. It doesn't fit my nephew. It's the wrong size.
	I want my money back [7] __________, please.
Do you have your receipt?	It's in here somewhere.
Don't worry about it. Take your money. [8] __________	

B ▶ Watch the video again and check your answers to Exercise A.

MILLY

SAM

NEENA

ZAC

GABY

USEFUL PHRASES

A Complete the useful phrases. Who says them, Milly (M) or the customer (C)?

about be must only over right

1 You're a yoga teacher, ______________? M / C
2 The sweaters are ______________ there. M / C
3 It says 'hand wash ______________' on the label. M / C
4 I have to ______________ quick. M / C
5 It ______________ be here! M / C
6 Don't worry ______________ it. M / C

B How do you say these useful phrases in your language?

PRONUNCIATION
Adding emphasis

9.7 **A** To emphasize a point, you can change the stressed word. Listen and underline the stressed word in each sentence.

1 a He is so special to me.
  b He is so special to me.
2 a My niece is really tall.
  b My niece is really tall.
3 a These shoes are very comfortable.
  b These shoes are very comfortable.
4 a You've been extremely helpful.
  b You've been extremely helpful.

9.7 **B** Listen again and repeat the sentences.

C **SPEAK** Work in pairs. Student A – say a sentence from Exercise A. Student B – point to the sentence. Take turns.

SPEAKING

A Work in pairs. Role-play buying a gift for your mother, father or best friend. Take turns being the customer and the sales clerk. Use the Functional language box to help you.

- Customer: Tell the sales clerk you want to buy a gift. Choose one of the items in the pictures. Ask for the price and for gift-wrapping.
- Sales clerk: Answer the customer's questions and sell the item.

B Role-play returning the gift you bought in Exercise A.

Customer: Tell the sales clerk you want to return something. Choose one of the following problems:

- it is the wrong size
- it is damaged
- the person you bought it for doesn't like it

Sales clerk: Listen to the customer and give them a refund.

Go shopping for clothes and ask for a refund

➤ Turn to **page XXVIII** to learn how to write a 'for sale' advertisement.

Unit 9 Review

VOCABULARY

A Complete the questions with the prepositions in the box.

by for from in ~~on~~ out of to up

1 What do you **spend** most money ___on___?
2 Do you ever **lend** money ________ your friends? Or **borrow** it ________ them?
3 How often do you **take money** ________ the ATM?
4 Do you **pay** ________ things mostly ________ **card**, cash or do you use your phone?
5 What kind of things do you pay for ________ **cash**?
6 What kind of things do you **save** ________ for?

B Complete the sentences with the correct form of *make* or *do*. Then finish the sentences so they are true for you.

1 I need to ___make___ **a decision** about *what to do on the weekend.*
2 I usually ________ **mistakes** when …
3 I ________ **a mess** when I was …
4 I usually ________ **my homework** …
5 I'd love to be able to ________ **a living** as a …
6 I ________ my friend **a favor** when …

GRAMMAR

A What would you do in these situations? Write sentences using the second conditional.

If I were you …

Get answers to your dilemmas.

1 The other day, I found a $100 bill in the street. What would you do? Would you keep it or take it to the police?

If I found a $100 bill in the street, I'd take it to the police.

2 I bought a phone from an online company, but they sent me two by mistake. What would you do? Would you tell them or keep both phones?

____

3 I am the best at math in my class. Some of my classmates want to give me money to copy my homework. What would you do? Would you accept the money or tell the teacher?

____

4 I saw someone who looked homeless steal some food from the local store that I shop at regularly. Would you offer to pay for the food for them or tell the store manager?

____

B Complete the news report with the adjective clauses in the box.

that Matt has hidden that is useful who finds one who has received a favor who needs food you don't know you spend it on

Man hiding money in Cardiff

A man from Cardiff in South Wales has hidden twenty £10 notes around the city (£10 is roughly $15). Anyone [1] ________ has to use the £10 to do something good for someone else. And this has to be someone [2] ________. The man behind the idea, Matt Callanan, says that you could give it to a person [3] ________ or, if it's raining when you find the note, you could buy something [4] ________, like an umbrella, and give it to someone! Callanan believes that a person [5] ________ will then do something good for someone else, and so on. So, if you find £10 [6] ________, you could be helping more than just the person [7] ________.

FUNCTIONAL LANGUAGE

Put the words in the correct order to complete the conversations.

Sales clerk:	[1]I / help / you / can / ? *Can I help you?*
Customer:	[2]for / I'm looking / for / a gift / my mother ________. It's her birthday.
Sales clerk:	[3]thing / kind / what / of / are you looking for / ? ________
Customer:	Well, maybe a scarf or some gloves … I like these gloves. [4]much / they / are / how / ? ________
Sales clerk:	Let me see. They're $20.
Customer:	Great. [5]them / I'll / take ________
Sales clerk:	[6]for / would you like me to / gift-wrap / you / them / ? ________
Customer:	Yes, please.
Sales clerk:	[7]like / you / how / would / pay, / to / cash or card / ? ________
Customer:	Card, please.
Sales clerk:	Thanks a lot!

10 SCIENCE AND TECHNOLOGY

Be less curious about people and more curious about ideas.

Marie Curie

Engineers of the future – two young Serbians work together to repair a robot.

OBJECTIVES

- describe and compare personal possessions
- describe types of technology
- discuss the requirements for a job
- make and receive formal and informal phone calls
- write a recommendation

Work with a partner. Discuss the questions.

1 Look at the picture. What were you curious about when you were a child?

2 What was your dream job when you were younger? Is it different now or the same?

3 What would you like to learn more about?

10.1 Devices

Describe and compare personal possessions

V electronic devices   G comparatives and superlatives   P /ɪst/ and superlative adjectives

VOCABULARY
Electronic devices

A SPEAK Work in pairs. Make a list of words to name or describe electronic devices. You have one minute.

A: Can you think of anything?
B: OK, a tablet and a cell phone.

B Go to the **Vocabulary Hub** on **page XXI**.

LISTENING

10.1 **A LISTEN FOR MAIN IDEA** Listen to four people talking about devices. What question are they answering?

a Which device do you use every day?
b What is the most useful device you own?
c What device do you most regret buying?

Glossary

package (n) an object or set of objects wrapped in a box or in paper and sent or given to someone
regret (v) to feel sorry or sad about something that has happened or about something you have said or done
reliable (adj) a reliable vehicle, piece of equipment or system always works well

10.1 **B LISTEN FOR DETAIL** Listen again and match the speakers (1–4) to the devices (a–h) they are describing. There are four devices you do not need.

a drone	___	e power bank	___
b e-reader	___	f tablet	___
c fitness tracker	___	g USB drive	___
d GPS	___	h laptop	___

C SPEAK Work in groups. Discuss the questions.

1 Which of the devices in the list in Exercise B do you own or would you like to own?
2 Which do you think is most useful and why?

GRAMMAR
Comparatives and superlatives

A Underline the comparative and superlative adjectives and adverbs in the sentences from the radio show.

1 My bag is a lot lighter than it used to be.
2 It's the best gadget I've ever bought.
3 I bought the cheapest one.
4 You can check words so much more quickly than in a paper dictionary.
5 This is definitely the most useful piece of technology I own.
6 It was more expensive than an old-fashioned paper map.
7 We spend a lot of time arguing about which turns the most quickly.

B WORK IT OUT Write the words you underlined in Exercise A in the correct place.

Comparatives and superlatives				
	Comparative	Example	Superlative	Example
one syllable adj	adjective + *-er* (+ *than*)	cheaper 1 ______	*the* + adjective + *-est*	the 4 ______ the lightest
adj with two + syllables	*more* + adjective (+ *than*)	more useful 2 ______	*the most* + adjective	the 5 ______ the most expensive
adj with two + syllables ending in -y	we cut the *-y* and add *-ier*	heavier easier	we cut the *-y* and add *- iest*	the heaviest the easiest
irregular adj	adjective (+ *than*)	better worse	*the* + adjective	the 6 ______ the worst
regular adv	*more* + adverb	more slowly 3 ______	*the most* + adverb	the most slowly 7 ______

C Look at the sentences and answer the questions.

1 'My bag is a lot lighter than it used to be.'
Which two words make the comparative adjective *lighter* stronger?

2 'You can check words so much more quickly.'
Which two words make the comparative adverb *quickly* stronger?

3 'Mine is a little heavier than some of the others because it has a camera.'
Which two words make the comparative adjective *heavy* weaker?

D Go to the **Grammar Hub** on **page XII**.

PRONUNCIATION
/ɪst/ and superlative adjectives

A Listen and repeat. 10.2

/ɪst/ heaviest, strongest, fastest

B Listen and underline the sound /ɪst/ in the sentences. Then listen and repeat. 10.3

1 The cheapest devices aren't the best.
2 The lightest laptop is better than the rest.
3 It's the fastest phone in our product test.

SPEAKING

A Work in groups. Show and describe your cell phone to the rest of the group. Use the questions to help you.

- When did you buy your phone? How old is it? How much was it? (If you don't mind saying!)
- How is it different from any other phones you have owned?
- What do you like about it?
- What don't you like about it?

B Use comparatives to compare your phones.

A: Jenny's phone is a little heavier than Marvin's.
B: Carly's phone was a lot more expensive than Mohammed's.

C Talk to the other groups in the class. Use superlatives to tell them about your group's phones.

A: Lucia's phone is the newest.
B: Fa's phone is the most interesting.

Describe and compare personal possessions

10.2 It's only good when it works

Describe types of technology

V using devices and the internet **G** more comparative structures **P** /əz/ in comparative structures

READING

A Complete the definitions (1–6) with the words in the box.

advertise (v) annoying (adj) mix (n) rely on (phr verb) security (n) symbol (n)

1 _______________ = making you feel slightly angry

2 _______________ = to trust someone or something to do a job or task for you

3 _______________ = a combination of different types of people who form a group, for example: *There was a good _______________ of people at the party.*

4 _______________ = to try to persuade people to buy a product or service by announcing it on television, on the internet, or in newspapers

5 _______________ = a picture or shape used to represent something: &*+@

6 _______________ = safety from attack, harm or damage

B Read the posts on the online forum *Is it just me?* Do you agree or disagree with the users' opinions?

	Agree	Disagree	Not sure
User 1			
User 2			
User 3			
User 4			

C Read again. Match the sentences to the users.

Which user …

1 says that other people might not have the same problem as they do? User 2

2 regularly forgets important personal information? __________

3 feels that technology is often unreliable? __________

4 thinks that people waste money on technology? __________

5 feels that it is important to protect your money online? __________

6 gets annoyed when trying to communicate online? __________

7 finds it hard to concentrate when using the internet? __________

D SPEAK Work in groups. What would you post on the site? Are the other students in your group annoyed by the same thing?

Is it just me? Tell the internet what annoys you and find out who agrees and who doesn't!

You say: People say technology and the internet have made life better. Sure, there are benefits, but there are also lots of annoying things. Does anyone agree?

The internet says:

(User 1) Dancingmaggie
I agree! The worst thing is how often things go wrong. Many times, when I try to make a video call, for example, the screen freezes. Video calls seem to fail as often as they work! Other things, too – you connect a drive and your computer crashes. You install a new app and everything stops working. Technology is only good when it works.

(User 2) RossM8
We rely on the internet, but we also waste time because of it. I'm usually searching for something online, but then I notice something interesting, click on a link and ten minutes later I'm reading about a cat that looks like Beyoncé or a man that married himself! Sometimes I forget what I was searching for in the first place. Some people are probably not as easily distracted as me.

(User 3) Aoneandatwo
The internet is amazing, and technology, too, in general. My problem is with the technology companies. They are always advertising new devices, so many people feel they have to own the latest model. If you ask me, the old models are usually just as good as the new ones, but, you know, 'your device is not as new as my device, so you're just not cool'. It annoys me that people stop using perfectly good phones and laptops.

(User 4) ABC123
I know online security is important, especially when it comes to your bank details, but trying to remember passwords is not as easy as it sounds. They usually have to be a mix of symbols, numbers and letters, and of course, you shouldn't write them down or use the same password on different websites. My memory is not reliable and I forget passwords as often as I remember them. I have blocked my accounts so many times!

Glossary

benefit (n) an advantage you get from a situation

distracted (adj) not able to concentrate on something

waste time (phrase) to spend time doing things that aren't important

VOCABULARY

Using devices and the internet

A Read *Is it just me?* again. Complete the collocations with verbs from the posts.

1 ___make___ **a video call** – use the internet to talk to and see someone else

2 ________ **your account** – if a bank or a social media provider does this, they stop your account from working because you have done something wrong

3 ________ **your password** – keep in your mind the secret word you chose to keep your email, bank or social media account safe

4 ________ **a drive** – add a small device with extra memory to your computer

5 ________ **on a link** – press the button on your mouse to connect quickly to a website

6 **your computer** ________ – your computer stops working; often you see a blue screen and a warning

7 **the screen** ________ – there's a problem that means the screen on your device won't change

8 ________ **an app** – add a new application to your phone or tablet

B SPEAK Work in groups. Discuss the questions.

1 What was the last really good app you installed on a device? Why do you like it?

2 How do you remember passwords? Have you ever blocked an account by entering the wrong password?

GRAMMAR

More comparative structures

A WORK IT OUT Look at the sentences from *Is it just me?* and choose the correct words to complete the rules.

If you ask me, the old models are usually ***just as good as*** *the new ones.*

Video calls seem to fail ***as often as*** *they work!*

Some people are probably ***not as easily distracted as*** *me.*

Comparative structures

1 To say that two things or people are ***the same*** / ***different*** in some way, we use (*just*) *as* + adjective/adverb + *as*.

2 To say that two things or people are ***the same*** / ***different*** in some way, we use *not as* + adjective/adverb + *as*.

B Match the sentences (1–4) with the correct meanings (a–d).

1 I don't get as annoyed with technology as my boyfriend does.

2 I get just as annoyed with technology as my boyfriend does.

3 I don't forget my passwords as often as my girlfriend does.

4 I forget my passwords just as often as my girlfriend does.

a We get equally annoyed with technology.

b He gets more annoyed with technology than me.

c She forgets her passwords more often than me.

d There is no difference in how often we forget our passwords.

C Go to the **Grammar Hub** on **page XII**.

PRONUNCIATION

/əz/ in comparative structures

10.4 **A** Listen to the sentences. How does each speaker pronounce *as*?

1 I don't think online banking is as secure as personal banking.

2 Sending an email is not as thoughtful as making a phone call.

10.4 **B** Listen again and repeat the conversation.

C SPEAK Work in pairs. Make similar conversations about these topics. Use *as … as* in its weak form.

1 going to the movie theater vs. watching movies online

2 paying in cash vs. paying by credit or debit card

3 shopping online vs. shopping in town

SPEAKING

Work in pairs. You are going to talk about different types of technology. Student A – go to the **Communication Hub** on **page XXIV**. Student B – go to the **Communication Hub** on **page XXIII**.

Describe types of technology

10.3 The best view in the universe

Discuss the requirements for a job

G need to | V collocations: science and research | P /ʊ/ and /uː/ | S facts and opinions

READING

A Work in pairs. Describe the picture. Try to use all the words in the box.

astronaut   Earth   International Space Station (ISS)   space   spacesuit   spacewalk   view

B SPEAK Work in groups. Discuss the questions.

1 What do you know about the history of human space travel?

2 What do you think would be the best and worst parts about visiting the ISS?

C READ FOR GIST Read the glossary and quickly read the article. Then choose the best subtitle.

1 A bridge to Mars

2 The laboratory in the stars

3 Just another day in space

INTERNATIONAL SPACE STATION

There are more than seven billion human beings living on Earth, and then there are a very special group of people who live somewhere completely different. Four hundred kilometers above us and circling the planet at 7.7 km per second, there are between six and ten astronauts who call the International Space Station (ISS) home.

Since the first crew members arrived in November 2000, records confirm that over 200 people from 18 countries have visited the ISS. Many only need to stay for a short time, but others need to spend several months there. So, what is the average zero-gravity day like on the ISS?

Living in space may seem exciting, but in fact, the daily routine is fairly repetitive. The crew needs to follow a detailed schedule. Days begin each morning at 6 am when, instead of an alarm clock, a different song chosen by the crew's families back on Earth is played to wake them up. As on Earth, the first stop is the bathroom. Keeping clean is difficult because without gravity everything floats, including water. Residents of the ISS report that washing your hair is particularly difficult in space.

After a challenging start comes breakfast. Almost all the food on the ISS is either dried or canned. Most people would agree that the daily menu is not one of the highlights of life in space. Next, it's time to exercise. Research has shown that muscles and bones quickly become weak in space, so astronauts need to work out for at least two hours each day, using special zero-gravity gym equipment.

The ISS is a large floating laboratory and astronauts spend much of the day doing research. Crew members work with scientists on Earth to do experiments and collect data, usually about the effects of space travel on the mind and body. It is thought that one day humans will travel to Mars, so astronauts test new technologies and look for solutions to the challenges of spending large amounts of time in space.

ISS crews have made many important discoveries. For example, they have proved that it is possible to grow a range of different vegetables to provide food in space. They have also found new ways to develop drugs to help treat diseases.

Crews also need to repair equipment and solve any problems with the station itself. Sometimes this means going outside. Because of the obvious risks, the astronauts spend weeks making preparations. Incredibly, it takes four hours just to put on a spacesuit before going out for a 'spacewalk'.

When they don't need to do any other tasks, the astronauts usually use their free time to contact relatives, read or watch movies. However, there is no doubt that the most popular activity is simply looking out of the window at what is probably the best view in the universe.

Glossary

crew (n) the people who work on a ship, aircraft, or space station

float (v) to move slowly through air

gravity (n) the force that makes objects fall to the ground

laboratory (n) a building or large room where people do scientific research

D READ FOR DETAIL Read again. Are the sentences fact (F) or opinion (O)? Use the information in the box to help you decide.

Facts and opinions

With so much written information online these days, it is important to question what you read. To do this, you need to recognize the difference between facts and opinions.
Facts are clearly true and usually presented with support.
Opinions are things that people believe, but may not be true.

Language regularly used to present facts

report, confirm, show, prove, find

There is no doubt that ...

Language often used to present opinions

seem, think, believe, feel, hope

Most people would agree that ...

1 There have been more than 200 visitors to the ISS. *F / O*
2 Life in space is exciting. *F / O*
3 It is hard to wash your hair when there is no gravity. *F / O*
4 The food on the ISS is not particularly enjoyable. *F / O*
5 The human body quickly loses strength in space. *F / O*
6 People will travel to Mars in the future. *F / O*
7 Plants can grow successfully in space. *F / O*
8 Research on the ISS is helping people with serious illnesses. *F / O*
9 The astronauts' favorite free time activity is looking down at Earth. *F / O*
10 There is no better view than the one from the ISS. *F / O*

E SPEAK Work in groups. Discuss the questions.

1 Would you visit the ISS if you had the chance? Why/Why not?
2 What would you miss most from Earth if you lived on the ISS for several months?

GRAMMAR
need to

A Look at the sentences from *International Space Station*. Choose the correct words to complete the rules.

The crew needs to follow a detailed schedule.

Crews also need to repair equipment and solve any problems with the station itself.

When they don't need to do any other tasks, the astronauts usually use their free time to contact relatives, read or watch movies.

need to

1 We use *need* to say something is ***possible / necessary***.
2 When *need* is followed by a verb, we use ***-ing / to*** + ***base form***.
3 We ***add / don't add*** -*s* to *need* when the subject is *he, she* or *it*.
4 We use the auxiliary ***do / have*** with negative and question forms of *need*.

B Go to the **Grammar Hub** on **page XII**.

VOCABULARY
Collocations: science and research

A Choose the correct verbs to complete the collocations in **bold** in the ISS schedule memo. Use *International Space Station* to help you.

ISS schedule memo 1174639 – Schedule number 4077

Good evening from Earth and the Control Center. As always, please [1]***do / follow*** tomorrow's **schedule** carefully.
9:00 am – IMPORTANT [2]***repair / solve*** broken gym **equipment**. This must be fixed today. Exercise program must return to normal.
10:00 am – Live link with University of Beijing – Give a presentation to students on Chinese astronauts who have [3]***made / found*** important **discoveries** on the ISS.
11:00 am – Continue [4]***testing / making* new technologies** for long-distance communication.
1:00 pm – Meeting to [5]***look for / collect* solutions** to the recent computer problems.
2:00 pm – Continue [6]***making / doing* research** into growing fruit in space. [7]***Do / Test* experiments**, numbers 146 to 149 and [8]***collect / follow*** more **data** on water levels.
5:00 pm – [9]***Make / Do*** more **preparations** for the next spacewalk. Try to [10]***test / solve*** the **problems** with spacesuit number 4.

B SPEAK Work in pairs. Go to the **Communication Hub** on **page XXV** and complete the survey. Then compare your results. Which of you would be best at working in space?

PRONUNCIATION
/ʊ/ and /uː/

10.5 **A** Listen to the word pairs. How is the pronunciation of the vowel sounds different?

1 foot food 2 woman routine

10.5 **B** Listen again and repeat the words.

10.6 **C** Write the words in the correct place in the table. Listen and check.

~~crew~~ group look move room would

/ʊ/	/uː/
	crew

10.6 **D** Listen again and repeat the words.

SPEAKING HUB

PREPARE You are going to talk about working in space. Go to the **Communication Hub** on **page XXIII** and follow the instructions.

Discuss the requirements for a job

Café Hub

10.4 Locked out

Ⓕ– make and receive formal and informal phone calls

Ⓟ– word stress and intonation

COMPREHENSION

A ▶ Cover the video screen. Listen to the video and put the events (a–j) in the correct order (1–10).

a The front door closes and locks shut. ___

b Gaby phones Neena's work. ___

c The signal is bad. ___

d Gaby is put on hold. ___

e Gaby phones Zac's mobile. ___

f Gaby leaves a voice message for Neena. ___

g It starts raining. ___

h Neena's phone is switched off. ___

i Gaby phones Neena's mobile. ___

j Gaby opens the front door to take the rubbish out. ___

Glossary

phones **(v) (British)** = calls **(v) (American)**
mobile **(n) (British)** = cell phone **(n) (American)**
rubbish **(n) (British)** = trash **(n) (American)**

B ▶ **SPEAK** Work in pairs. Predict the answers to the questions. Then watch the video and check your answers.

1. Where is Gaby?
2. How does Gaby get locked out?
3. Where is Zac?
4. Where is Neena?
5. What is the music we hear three times?
6. How does the video end?

MILLY

SAM

NEENA

ZAC

GABY

FUNCTIONAL LANGUAGE

Make and receive formal and informal phone calls

A Write the words in the correct order to make useful phrases. Then write each phrase in the correct place.

1 up / breaking / You're / .

You're breaking up.

2 you / hear / can't / I / .

____

3 me / Can / you / hear / ?

____

4 cut / out / You / again / .

____

5 that / What / was / ?

____

6 very / The / isn't / signal / good / .

____

Describe a phone problem	Ask for clarification
You're breaking up.	

B Complete the receptionist's replies with two of the words in the box.

just over soon through

Receptionist: Good morning. You're [1]__________ to Jobs, Jobs, Jobs and Jobs. How can I help?

Gaby: Hello, is it possible to speak to Neena Patel?

Receptionist: Yes, of course. I'll [2]__________ try to put you [3]__________. I'm afraid the line is busy. Would you like to hold?

Gaby: Yes, please.

[MUSIC ON HOLD]

Receptionist: Thank you for calling. [4]__________ putting you [5]__________.

C **SPEAK** Work in pairs. Practice the conversation in Exercise B with your own ideas.

PRONUNCIATION

Word stress and intonation

10.7 **A** Listen and repeat Amelia's voicemail greeting. Copy the word stress and intonation.

Amelia: Hi, this is Amelia Jones. I can't take your call at the moment. Please leave a message after the beep.

B **SPEAK** Work in pairs. You are going to record your own voicemail greeting in English.

- Practice your voicemail greeting.
- Record your voicemail greeting on your phone.
- Call your partner and listen to his/her greeting.
- Leave a message for your partner.

SPEAKING

Work in groups. Choose a problem from the box or use your own ideas. Then role-play calling two friends to ask for help. Use the Functional Language box to help you.

You've locked yourself out. You've lost your car keys. You've lost your house keys. You've missed the last bus home. You've forgotten your passport.

Student A: Call a friend (Student B). The signal is bad.

Student B: Answer Student A. The signal is bad.

Student A: Call another friend at Jones & Jones. You can't get through. You speak to Student C (the receptionist).

Student C: You are the receptionist at Jones & Jones. Answer Student A. The line is busy.

Student A: Answer Student C (the receptionist).

Make and receive formal and informal phone calls

➤ Turn to page XXIX to learn how to write a recommendation.

Unit 10 Review

VOCABULARY

A Choose the correct words to complete the sentences.

1. My new ***drone*** / ***fitness tracker*** has arrived. Should we go to the park and fly it?
2. I'm so bad at directions – this ***USB drive*** / ***GPS*** is really useful!
3. I think a ***fitness tracker*** / ***tablet*** would make me exercise more.
4. I always take my ***e-reader*** / ***power bank*** on vacation with me. I love books.
5. My son wants a ***drone*** / ***tablet*** so he can watch his favorite TV shows.
6. A ***GPS*** / ***USB drive*** is very useful when I go on business trips. I can take my work everywhere!
7. I don't know what I would do without my ***power bank*** / ***e-reader*** – my phone battery is always running out.

B Complete the information with the verbs in the box. You need to use one of the verbs twice.

collect do look make test

Higgerfield University
SCIENCE DEPARTMENT

Why study science at Higgerfield?

We asked three first-year students why they chose science subjects.

Sergei: I want to [1] __________ data and [2] __________ for solutions to the problem of climate change.

Masha: I want to [3] __________ research on space travel and [4] __________ new technologies to help get us to other planets.

Melissa: I want to [5] __________ discoveries and [6] __________ experiments that will help save people's lives.

To find out more about studying Science at Higgerfield, join us at one of our open houses.

GRAMMAR

A Complete the article with comparative and superlative forms of the missing adjectives and adverbs.

Hi-fi & Wi-fi Magazine **Awards**

Cell phones

1st Chitchat 8
2nd Speakup 4 3rd Talkabout 2

Overall

The Talkabout 2 is a good phone, but the Speakup 4 is [1] ___better___. And this year, the Chitchat 8 is [2] ___the best___.

Is it reliable?

The Talkabout 2 is fairly reliable, but the Speakup 4 is [3] __________. Again, the Chitchat 8 is [4] __________.

Is it easy to use?

The Talkabout 2 is fairly easy to use, but the Speakup 4 is definitely [5] __________ to use. However, the Chitchat 8 is [6] __________ to use.

Does it charge quickly?

The Talkabout 2 charges quickly, but the Speakup 4 charges [7] __________. Again, the Chitchat 8 wins this year because it charges [8] __________.

B Add *as … as* to complete each sentence.

1. I get just (as) annoyed with pop-up ads (as) anybody else.
2. That messaging service is not private this one.
3. My wife doesn't forget passwords easily I do.
4. My dad's phone is just old-fashioned my mom's.
5. I don't learn how to use new devices quickly I used to when I was young.
6. This game is just good the other soccer games on the market.

FUNCTIONAL LANGUAGE

Complete the words in the phone conversation. The first letter of each word has been given to help you.

Derek: Hello, this is Derek Lebarge. [1]Sorry, I can't t______ your call at the m______. [2]Please leave a m______ after the b______.

Murray: Derek? Derek? It's Murray. [3]Sorry, the s______ isn't very g______. [4]What was t______? [5]You're b______ up. Hello?

11 NATURAL WORLD

An urban fox begins his nightly hunt for food, Twickenham, United Kingdom.

OBJECTIVES

- talk about natural wonders
- read and talk about wildlife photography
- talk about the causes and effects of plastic pollution
- tell a story
- write an email giving suggestions and advice

Work with a partner. Discuss the questions.

1 Do you find the city or the country more relaxing? Why?

2 Read the quote. Do you agree with Muir?

3 Look at the picture. What wildlife is there in your city?

11.1 Natural wonders

Talk about natural wonders

V natural features **P** /e/ and /iː/ **G** the passive voice (simple present and simple past)

VOCABULARY
Natural features

A Label the pictures (1–7) with the words in the box.

canyon harbor lights mountain reef volcano waterfall

B Go to the **Vocabulary Hub** on **page XXI**.

C **SPEAK** Work in pairs. Name other examples of the natural features in Exercise A and in the Vocabulary Hub.

A: Well, there's Mount Fuji and The Great Barrier Reef. But I can't think of a famous canyon.

B: What about The Grand Canyon in Arizona?

PRONUNCIATION
/e/ and /iː/

11.1 **A** Listen to the vowel sounds /e/ and /iː/. What is the vowel sound in each word in the box? Write the words in the correct place.

be get leave met reef rest see ten

/e/	/iː/

11.2 **B** Listen and check your answers. Then listen again and repeat the words.

LISTENING

A The places in the pictures above have recently been named as the *Seven Natural Wonders of the World*. Match the names (a–g) with the pictures (1–7). What do you know about them?

a Mount Everest *4*
b Great Barrier Reef ___
c Grand Canyon ___
d Northern lights (aurora borealis) ___
e Rio de Janeiro harbor ___
f Victoria Falls ___
g Paricutin volcano ___

11.3 **B** **LISTEN FOR KEY WORDS** Listen to a radio travel show about the *Seven Natural Wonders of the World*. In which order did the travel writer visit the places?

1 *the Great Barrier Reef*
2 ___
3 ___
4 ___
5 ___
6 ___
7 ___

Glossary

coral (n) a very small ocean creature that lives in large groups that look like plants, in places where the water is warm
crater (n) the round hole at the top of a volcano
form (v) to make something exist
promote (v) to support something
unique (adj) not the same as anything else

11.3 **C LISTEN FOR DETAIL** Listen to the radio show again and answer the questions.

1 What is the goal of the Seven Natural Wonders organization?

2 What three main factors were used to choose the Seven Natural Wonders?

3 Why did Mike decide to visit the Seven Natural Wonders?

4 Which of the seven natural wonders …

a is visible only at certain times of the year? ______________________

b was formed the most recently? ______________________

c is located in two countries? ______________________

d is famous for its different colors? ______________________

e is the highest? ______________________

f is the most visited? ______________________

D SPEAK Work in pairs. Which of the Seven Natural Wonders you would most like to visit and why?

GRAMMAR

The passive voice (simple present and simple past)

A WORK IT OUT Look at the sentences from the radio show about the seven natural wonders. Then complete the rules using the words in the box.

1 The decision **was based** on three main things.

2 The places **were chosen** according to how unique the place is …

3 It's **made** of over 400 different kinds of coral.

4 It **was** only **formed** in 1943.

5 The canyon **was created** by the Colorado River.

6 It's **visited** by about four-and-a-half million people a year.

be *by* do not say past participle

The passive voice (simple present and simple past)

1 We make the passive voice with the auxiliary verb ______________ + the ______________ of the main verb.

2 We most commonly use the passive voice when we ______________ who or what performs or causes the action. This is usually because the person or thing is not known, not important or obvious.

3 We sometimes use the passive voice with an agent (the person or thing that performs or causes the action). We use ______________ to introduce the agent.

B Go to the **Grammar Hub** on **page XIV**.

C SPEAK Work in pairs. Test your general knowledge! Make sentences about these natural wonders using a word from each column. Discuss what you know about each place.

Jeju Island is located off the coast of South Korea.

1 Jeju Island	form	around 30 million people a year
2 The White Cliffs of Dover	locate	40–50 million years ago
3 The Himalayas	visit	as Ayers Rock
4 The Niagara Falls	make	off the coast of South Korea
5 Uluru in Australia	discover	of chalk and similar minerals
6 The Galapagos Islands	also/know	the Bishop of Panama in 1535

SPEAKING

11.4 **A** Listen to a presentation about the Gullfoss Waterfall in Iceland and answer the questions.

- Where is it located?
- When was it formed or created?
- What is it surrounded by?
- How is it reached?
- Who and how many people visit it?
- Why are people attracted to it?

B Work in pairs. Choose a natural wonder in your country or continent to give a presentation about. Use the questions in Exercise A to help you.

C Give your presentation to the class.

Talk about natural wonders

11.2 Animal images

Read and talk about wildlife photography

V animals **G** adjective + infinitive **P** *to* /tə/

VOCABULARY

Animals

A SPEAK Work in pairs. Make a list of animals. You have one minute.

B Go to the **Vocabulary Hub** on **page XXI**.

C SPEAK Work in pairs. Write down your three favorite animals. Tell your partner what you wrote. Explain your choices.

D SPEAK Work in pairs. Go to the **Communication Hub** on **page XXII** to see what your answers to Exercise C mean. Do you agree or disagree?

My first animal is a dolphin. I think I'm like a dolphin because it's smart, moves quickly, is very sociable and always in groups.

READING

A Match the words and phrases (1–5) with the definitions (a–e).

1 habitat
2 wildlife
3 make eye contact
4 facial expression
5 life cycle

a the series of changes that happen to an animal or plant during its life
b the look on someone's face that shows what their thoughts or feelings are
c animals, birds and plants that live in natural conditions
d the type of place that a particular animal usually lives in or a particular plant usually grows in
e situation in which two people look at each other's eyes

Behind the lens: Anthony Remy, wildlife photographer

You may not know Anthony Remy's name but you will almost certainly have seen one of his photos. He spoke to us about his 30-year career close-up with wildlife.

Where did your interest in wildlife photography come from?
I grew up in Canada with nature right on my doorstep. I just had to step outside and I could see all manner of mammals, reptiles, birds and amphibians. One day my older cousin, Julian, took me to see a grizzly fishing with her cub … from a safe distance, of course. Julian passed me his camera so that I could zoom in. It was great to watch them so closely, I never wanted to forget it. I pressed the shutter and that's when I decided what I wanted to do for the rest of my life.

Is it easy to find work? I imagine it's fairly difficult.
It is at first when no one knows your name and you don't have any contacts at magazines. Over time your reputation grows. You ask local stores to put up framed photos or sell some of your cards … you know, anything to make a living!

I guess you're asked this a lot but what's your favorite animal?
Well … I love dogs … I have four at home. In terms of photography though orangutans without a doubt. Their name literally means 'person of the forest' in Malay and you can see why. It's not just their body language and facial expressions that are so like ours, but also their social interactions. Over my career I've also taken a lot of photos of spiders, which you may not understand! But most people come to realize, like me, that up close they are unexpectedly fascinating.

And which animal don't you enjoy taking photos of?
Well some animals are so 'seen' there are hundreds of photographs of them … you know, elephants, eagles, tigers. It isn't easy to take something amazing that everyone would be interested in. Certain types of monkeys are challenging too as they don't want to make eye contact with people. Then there are lemurs which will look you in the eye, in fact they'll climb all over you, but they live deep in the Madagascan rainforest. Habitats like that are hard to get to, especially carrying camera equipment.

So any top tips for future wildlife photographers out there?
Don't rush out and spend a fortune on a new camera. It really isn't the most important thing. An interest in animals is obvious but essential. Unless you are incredibly lucky, be prepared for uncomfortable hours or even weeks waiting for the perfect shot. Researching habitats and life cycles can certainly help this. If you watch an animal for long enough, you can predict its behavior. For example, I always know when a grizzly will swipe for the salmon and so I am there ready to capture the moment.

Glossary

body language (n) the movements or positions of your body that show others what you are thinking or feeling
close-up (n) a picture of someone or something taken from a position very near them
make a living (phrase) to earn money from a job

B SCAN Read *Behind the lens* and answer the questions.

Which animal(s) …

1 did Anthony Remy first take pictures of?
2 is/are his favorite to photograph?
3 is/are difficult to get a good picture of?
4 does he think has/have predictable behavior?

C READ FOR DETAIL Choose the correct answers, a, b or c.

1 Anthony Remy started taking pictures of bears …
  a to show his cousin what he had seen.
  b to help him remember them.
  c to capture the beauty of where he is from.
2 He thinks orangutans are …
  a shy. b dangerous.
  c similar to humans.
3 He thinks his pictures of spiders usually …
  a surprise people. b frighten people.
  c disappoint people.
4 He thinks some animals, such as elephants …
  a are not interesting to photograph.
  b don't do anything surprising.
  c have been photographed too much.
5 He says monkeys …
  a don't like to look at humans.
  b try to hide from humans.
  c behave like humans.
6 In Anthony's opinion, it is not necessary …
  a to know about the animals you are photographing.
  b to spend time watching and have a lot of patience.
  c to have a lot of expensive camera equipment.

D SPEAK Work in pairs. Discuss the skills and characteristics you need to be a wildlife photographer.

GRAMMAR
Adjective + infinitive

A WORK IT OUT Look at the sentences from *Behind the lens*. Add the missing adjective + infinitive. Then complete the rule.

1 It was ____________________ them so closely …
2 It isn't ____________________ something amazing that everyone would be interested in.
3 Habitats like that are ____________________ to, especially carrying camera equipment.

Adjective + infinitive

When a verb comes after an adjective, we use the ______________ form of the verb.

B Go to the **Grammar Hub** on **page XIV**.

C SPEAK Go to the **Communication Hub** on **page XXV** and follow the instructions.

PRONUNCIATION
to /tə/

11.5 **A** Listen to the weak pronunciation of *to* /tə/ in the sentences.

1 It's easy to take a good picture.
2 It's important to be patient.
3 Are you ready to leave?

11.5 **B** Listen again and repeat the sentences.

SPEAKING

A Read the tips about what makes a good animal picture. Do you agree? Add a tip of your own.

✓ It's important to show the animal in its natural habitat.
✓ It's important to be able to see the animal's face and eyes. It gives an idea of how the animal is feeling or what it's thinking.
✓ It's good to photograph the animal doing something. It's even better to catch it doing something unusual or maybe something funny.
✓ A good animal picture shows detail and color that you don't normally see.
✓ A good picture is one where you see something new. You learn something about the animal.

B Look at the pictures (a–f) above and answer the questions.

- Which of the features in the tips above does each picture have?
- Choose the best animal picture in your opinion.
- Put the others in order of second favorite, third favorite.

C Work in groups. Compare your ideas. In your group, decide on the best animal picture.

Read and talk about wildlife photography

11.3 Throw-away world

Talk about the causes and effects of plastic pollution

P /l/ pronounced and silent **G** *even* **V** *somewhere, nowhere, everywhere, anywhere*
S looking for ways of expressing cause and effect

READING

A Work in pairs. Discuss the questions.

1 Do you recycle? What kind of things do you recycle? Is it easy to recycle things where you live? What happens to things you throw away that are not recycled?

2 Look at the picture. What can you see on the beach? How do you think it got there?

B READ FOR GIST Read *The nightmare of Plastic Island* and decide which is the best summary.

a Plastic is usually blown into the ocean and is carried around the world by ocean currents. The pictures of Henderson Island show how we should clean the beaches before the plastic enters the ocean.

b Plastic is carried to certain parts of the world by ocean currents, but it does not reach other parts of the world. The pictures of Henderson Island suggest that the situation is worse than it actually is.

c Plastic is carried around the world by ocean currents and reaches the most remote beaches and other places. The pictures of Henderson Island show how serious the problem is.

C READ FOR DETAIL Answer the questions. Use the information in the box to help you. Then read again and check your answers.

Looking for ways of expressing cause and effect

Look for verbs, linking words and nouns that express cause and effect:

- **verbs:** *This **means** there are … This has **led** to …*
- **linking words:** *This is **because** … **Because of** this, … **If** we do this, …*
- **nouns:** *And as **a result**, …*

1 Why is there plastic everywhere?

2 Why was plastic successful when it first appeared?

3 Scientists believe that there are five trillion pieces of plastic in the oceans. What is this number based on?

4 Some marine animals eat plastic. How can this affect humans?

5 Experts believe plastic pollution in the oceans is a serious problem. How have some governments responded to this?

6 What can individuals do to help reduce the amount of plastic pollution?

The nightmare of PLASTIC ISLAND

Plastic is everywhere. It is at the bottom of the oceans, on tropical beaches and at the top of Mount Everest. It is even on the surface of Mars. This is because each year, over 300 million metric tons of plastic is produced, used and then most of it is thrown away.

Plastic was invented over 100 years ago. When it first appeared, it was an instant success. It was cheap, convenient, had many uses and was long-lasting. And that is the problem. Plastic will not go away. It may break into smaller and smaller pieces, but every piece of plastic ever made still exists somewhere in the world.

Up to 12 million metric tons of plastic enters the world's oceans every year. This means there are around five trillion pieces of plastic currently in our oceans. Once there, it can be carried by the currents for many years and travel thousands of kilometers. Some of it is eaten by marine wildlife and enters the food chain. As a result, thousands of pieces of marine plastic are consumed by humans each year when they eat fish and other seafood. However, most of the plastic in the seas and oceans eventually washes up on beaches. Nowhere on Earth has as much plastic as the beaches of Henderson Island in the South Pacific. The remote island is the most polluted anywhere in the world, and 99.8 percent of this pollution is plastic. The island's beaches contain around 38 million pieces of plastic; most of this is from everyday consumer goods.

Henderson Island is a UNESCO World Heritage site and it is an important habitat for wildlife. Jennifer Lavers, of the University of Tasmania, says that the situation on Henderson Island shows that 'nowhere is safe from plastic pollution'. She even believes that marine plastic pollution is 'as important as climate change'. Other experts describe the situation as 'a major ecological disaster' and 'an environmental emergency'.

Because of this, there is a global effort to reduce the amount of plastic pollution. For example, Indonesia has promised to spend up to $1 billion on reducing plastic and other waste products which pollute its waters. This has led to other governments making similar pledges.

However, the best way to prevent trash from washing up on beaches would be for us as individuals to use less plastic, especially things that we don't even need. These are single-use and 'disposable' items, such as cutlery and even toothbrushes. We should also buy products with less packaging and recycle more. If we do this, we will reduce the amount of plastic that ends up in our oceans and on our beaches. We will also be less likely to find plastic returning to us on our dinner plates.

Glossary

consumer goods (n) things you buy for personal or home use, such as food and clothing
current (n) a strong movement of water in one direction
marine (adj) living or happening in the ocean
remote (adj) far away from other cities, towns or people

PRONUNCIATION
/l/ pronounced and silent

11.6 **A** Listen to the words. Is the letter *l* pronounced in each word?

1 plastic	3 smaller	5 calm	7 should
2 travel	4 would	6 climate	8 folk

11.7 **B** Work in pairs. Write the words in the correct place. Listen and check.

l is pronounced	*l* is not pronounced

C SPEAK Work in pairs. Why is the letter *l* pronounced in some words and not in others?

GRAMMAR
even

A WORK IT OUT Look at the phrases from *The nightmare of Plastic Island*. Then choose the correct words to complete the rules.

It is even on the surface of Mars.

She even believes that marine plastic pollution is 'as important as climate change.'

… especially things that we don't even need.

These are single-use and 'disposable' items, such as cutlery and even toothbrushes.

even

1. We use *even* to suggest that something is ***surprising* / *obvious***.
2. We use *even* ***before* / *after*** verbs, but ***before* / *after*** auxiliary verbs (*be, have, can, don't*).
3. We ***can* / *cannot*** use *even* before nouns.

B Go to the **Grammar Hub** on **page XIV**.

C SPEAK Work in groups. Tell your group three things that you think are surprising. You can talk about natural wonders, animals or pollution. Use *even* and *don't even*.

VOCABULARY
somewhere, nowhere, everywhere, anywhere

A Complete the sentences from *The nightmare of Plastic Island* with *somewhere, nowhere, everywhere* or *anywhere*. Then read again and check your answers.

1. Plastic is ________________.
2. Every piece of plastic ever made still exists ________________ in the world.
3. ________________ on Earth has as much plastic as the beaches of Henderson Island.
4. The remote island is the most polluted ________________ in the world.
5. Jennifer Lavers says that '________________ is safe from plastic pollution'.

B Complete the sentences with *somewhere, nowhere, everywhere* or *anywhere*.

1. I'd like to live by the ocean – ideally, ________________ near a big sandy beach and without too many people.
2. There is ________________ like India. It's unique. There's a lot of pollution and poverty, but it's an amazing place. ________________ you go, you see something incredible.
3. If I could visit ________________ in the world, I'd go to California. I've always wanted to go there. If not California, I'd like to go ________________ similar with big cities, lots of beaches and warm weather.
4. I was very impressed by Singapore. ________________ was so clean. There was no trash ________________.

C SPEAK Rewrite the sentences in Exercise B using your own ideas. Then work in pairs and share your ideas. Ask questions to find out more information.

I'd like to live in a town – ideally, somewhere with a few stores and surrounded by nice countryside.

SPEAKING HUB

A You are going to do the Plastic Challenge. Read about the Plastic Challenge, which is organized by the Marine Conservation Society.

The Plastic Challenge asks people to stop using plastic items for as long as they can. This could be for a day, a week or a month. Our message is 'reduce, reuse, recycle'. We're challenging people to give up their single-use plastics, such as prepackaged sandwiches, prepackaged meals, bottled drinks and so on. Do the Plastic Challenge and you'll never look at your grocery shopping in the same way again!

B PLAN Spend a few minutes thinking about the following.

1. Make a list of all the plastic you have used …
   a. today.
   b. in the last week.
   c. How much of this was single-use items?
2. Imagine you are going to do the Plastic Challenge.
   a. Which items would be easier to stop using and which would be more difficult?
   b. What changes would you need to make in your daily life to do the challenge?
   c. How long do you think you could do the challenge for?

C DISCUSS Work in groups.

1. Compare and discuss your lists and your ideas about the Plastic Challenge.
2. Decide on a plan for doing the Plastic Challenge. You must agree to do the same things.

Talk about the causes and effects of plastic pollution

11.4 Power cut

F– tell a story P– showing interest

COMPREHENSION

A ▶ 00:00–03:33 **Watch the first part of the video and answer the questions.**

1 What is a 'power cut'? What is the American English word for this?
2 What kind of story does Sam tell Neena and Gaby?
3 How do Neena and Gaby feel as Sam tells the story?
4 How do you think Sam's story ends?

B ▶ 03:33–04:29 **Watch the second part of the video. Compare the end of Sam's story with your ideas in Exercise A. Is it a good story?**

C ▶ **Work in pairs. Put the events of Sam's story in the correct order (1–10). Then watch the video again and check your answers.**

a After that, I tried to switch the lights on, but there was no power. ___
b I wasn't alone. ___
c It was stormy. Very stormy. ___
d I arrived back at my uncle's house, got out of the car and walked up to the front door. ___
e So anyway, I went inside and called out to see if my uncle was home. 'Uncle Mike' I shouted – there was no answer. ___
f It all started on a stormy night when I was in Cornwall staying with my uncle. ___
g I walked into the kitchen and sat down in the dark. My uncle was missing – I was scared. ___
h I pushed the door and the wind blew it open. ___
i In the end, I sat there alone in the dark. ___
j Then the front door slammed shut behind me. ___

D Match Sam's sentences (1–5) with the replies (a–e).

1 This reminds me of a very scary experience I once had.
2 It all started on a stormy night when I was in Cornwall staying with my uncle.
3 Can I continue my story now?
4 I was scared.
5 My phone was dead.

a Where is Cornwall?
b You poor thing!
c How awful!
d So, tell us. What happened?
e Sure. Go on.

MILLY

SAM

NEENA

ZAC

GABY

FUNCTIONAL LANGUAGE

Tell a story

A Look at the underlined words in Comprehension Exercises C and D. Complete the box with one of the words.

Tell a story and listen to a story
Give background information
It was [1] ______________ */windy/raining.*
The sun was shining and it was hot.
Use linking phrases
Beginning: *At first … / To start with … / It all* [2] ______________ …
Middle: *Then … / After* [3] ______________ … / *So* [4] ______________, …
End: *In the* [5] ______________, …
Say how you felt
I was excited/surprised/worried/relieved/frightened/ [6] ______________.
Keep the story going
Go on. / So, [7] ______________ us. *(Then) What happened?*
Respond to dramatic events
You [8] ______________ */lucky thing.*
How [9] ______________ */frightening/funny.*
That's terrible/awful/funny.

B SPEAK Work in pairs. You are going to practice responding to events.

1 Look at the responses in the box. Choose three responses you want your partner to give. Circle them.

> How awful/frightening/funny. That's terrible/awful/funny. You poor/lucky thing.

2 Write down three things you could tell your partner to get him/her to give those responses.

3 Tell your partner your ideas. How does he/she respond?

Student A wants Student B to say 'You lucky thing'.

A: I found $5 in the street this morning.
B: You lucky thing!

Glossary

power cut **(n) (British)** = power outage **(n) (American)**
torch **(n) (British)** = flashlight **(n) (American)**

PRONUNCIATION

Showing interest

11.8 **A** Listen and write how the responses sound in the correct place.

Very interested	Not very interested
That's awful.	

11.8 **B** Listen again and repeat the responses.

C SPEAK Work in pairs. Practice saying the responses. Listen to your partner and say whether he/she sounds very interested or not very interested.

SPEAKING

A Work in pairs. You are going to tell your partner a story. Choose one of the topics or use your own ideas. Include background information, linking phrases and say how you felt.

A time when … you got lost / you lost your keys / you met an old friend / you won a prize / something happened on vacation.

B Tell each other your stories and react and respond appropriately.

A: I lost some car keys once.
B: That's awful!
A: I was on vacation with the family in Menorca …
B: Where is Menorca?

Tell a story

➤ Turn to **page XXX** to learn how to write an email giving suggestions and advice.

Unit 11 Review

VOCABULARY

A Complete the sentences using a word from box a and box b.

a Amazon Atlas Death Grand Lascaux Panama ~~Sahara~~ San Francisco

b Bay Canal Canyon Caves ~~Desert~~ Mountains Rainforest Valley

1 The *Sahara Desert* is 9.3 million square kilometers, which is almost the same size as China.
2 The ______________ stretch for 2,500 km in Morocco, Algeria and Tunisia.
3 The Golden Gate Bridge is 2,737 meters long and crosses the ______________.
4 The ______________ is 446 km in length and 29 km across at its widest point.
5 The ______________ is 9.3 million square kilometers and is located in nine countries in South America.
6 In 1913, a temperature of 56.7°C was recorded in ______________ in eastern California.
7 The ______________ connects the Atlantic Ocean with the Pacific Ocean.
8 The walls of the ______________ in southwestern France are decorated with 17,000-year-old paintings of animals, such as cows, horses and deer.

B Find 17 animals and write them in the correct place.

Mammals	Birds	Reptiles	Insects	Fish
bear				

C Choose the correct words to complete the sentences.

1 Plastic is ***anywhere / everywhere***. It has more forms and uses than any other material on the planet.
2 About 30 percent of all the plastic ever made is still in use ***anywhere / somewhere*** in the world today.
3 Recycling rates of plastic are not the same ***somewhere / everywhere*** in the world. For example, in Europe about 30 percent is recycled, in China around 25 percent and in the US the figure is just 10 percent.
4 There is almost ***anywhere / nowhere*** on Earth that does not have plastic pollution.

GRAMMAR

A Complete the text with the correct passive form of the verbs in parentheses. Add *by* where it is needed.

Ayers Rock [1] ____________ (*locate*) in the Uluru-Kata Tjuta National Park in central Australia. It [2] ____________ (*also / know*) as Uluru, which is its original Aboriginal name. The rock [3] ____________ (*form*) over 600 million years ago and it [4] ____________ (*originally / locate*) under the ocean. The summit is generally flat but, there are valleys and caves that [5] ____________ (*create*) the wind and rain over millions of years.

B Complete the conversations with the words in the box.

easy/use lucky/see necessary/have safe/drink unusual/see

1 **A:** Is your camera ________________?
B: Yes, it's very easy. Anyone can use it.
2 **A:** It isn't ________________ the water here.
B: OK, I'll get some bottled water.
3 **A:** It isn't ________________ expensive equipment to take good pictures.
B: I agree. A creative eye is all you need.
4 **A:** It's ________________ the northern lights at this time of year.
B: Yes, we were very ________________ them.

C Rewrite the sentences with the correct form of *even / don't even*.

1 I use plastic bags. (*not even*)

____

2 Ella does a lot of recycling; she recycles clothes. (*even*)

____

3 I never buy plastic. I let my children play with plastic toys. (*not even*)

____

FUNCTIONAL LANGUAGE

Add the missing words to complete the conversation.

A: It all [1]**s**__ __ __ __ __ __ when we decided to walk along the Samaria Gorge in Crete.
B: [2]**G**__ on.
A: Well, Sandy, my friend, didn't want to do it. It's a fairly long and steep walk to get down in the gorge. But she finally agreed to it.
B: So, what [3]**h**__ __ __ __ __ __ __ __?
A: After about two hours, Sandy fell over and hurt her leg.
B: Oh, no! [4]**H**__ __ awful! [5]**P**__ __ __ thing!
A: So, [6]**a**__ __ __ __ __, she took some painkillers and decided to go back to the hotel.
B: [7]**T**__ __ __ what happened?
A: Well her leg was broken …
B: [8]**T**__ __ __' __ terrible.
A: Yes, but in the [9]**e**__ __, everything was OK.

12 MEDIA

A printer works through the night to get out the news on time.

> I do not take a single newspaper, nor read one a month, and I feel happier for it.
>
> Thomas Jefferson

OBJECTIVES

- talk about the pros and cons of online news
- talk and debate about different TV viewing habits
- talk about advertising and what makes a good advertisement
- give and respond to opinions
- write a story

Work with a partner. Discuss the questions.

1 How often do you read the news?

2 Look at the picture. Do you think newspapers will exist in the future?

3 Do you think 24-hour news on TV and the internet is a positive thing? Why/Why not?

12.1 The news

● Talk about the pros and cons of online news

V news expressions G reported speech P /ɒ/, /ɔː/ and /oʊ/

VOCABULARY

News expressions

A Replace the words in **bold** with the words and phrases with the same meaning in the box.

breaking news follow ~~get~~ journalist news headlines report share

1 How do you generally ~~**watch / listen to**~~ ___get___ the news? TV? Radio? Online?
2 How closely do you **pay attention to** ______________ the news?
3 What are the current **biggest news stories** ______________?
4 How do you usually find out about **the very latest news** ______________?
5 How often do you **repost** ______________ news stories on social media?
6 What characteristics and qualities do you need to be a **person who writes about the news** ______________?
7 Do different news organizations **communicate** ______________ the news in different ways? How?

B Work in pairs. Ask and answer the questions in Exercise A.

READING

A READ FOR GIST Read the article and choose the best subtitle. Give reasons.

a here and now b good or bad?
c past and present d truth or lies?

B READ FOR DETAIL Read again and answer the questions.

1 Today, what are the main ways we get our news?
2 Do people trust newspapers, radio and TV news more or less than online news sites?
3 Why is there less control over the quality of journalism today than in the past?
4 What is fake news and what is the main reason for it?
5 Why is it usually difficult to know if something is fake news or not?
6 What can help us to decide if a news story is fake or not?

C SPEAK Work in pairs. Discuss the questions.

1 What are the pros and cons of online news?
2 Do you think fake news is a problem? Why/Why not?

The news: ______________

Not long ago, television, radio and newspapers were the main ways of receiving the latest news. But the way we get our news today is very different. Most of us have mobile devices and the internet is available almost everywhere. As a result, online news sites and social media give us quick and easy access to what is going on in the world. Headlines change constantly, we get breaking news as it happens and we can follow the latest developments minute by minute.

Most people still believe traditional media more than news found online – stating that online articles tend to have a very one-sided view. When questioned further one person said they thought the news was usually unreliable or that they did not trust it. In contrast, those who get their news from the TV, radio or paper said that 'fake' or biased news was not really a concern. This lack of trust in online news is mostly because it is so easy for anyone to set up a website and report the news. This means there is less control over online journalism, and separating fact from fiction is becoming more difficult.

'Fake news' has become a familiar term. It describes invented news stories that are designed to seem real. Fake stories are usually used for political reasons or to support some other way of thinking. There were a number of famous fake news stories, for example, during the 2016 United States presidential election. Some fake news websites are designed to look like genuine news sites and have similar web addresses, for example ABCnews.nett. Also, the fake news stories are usually mixed in with real stories, which makes it difficult to notice them.

So, how do we know if a story is fake or not? First, check the source of the story. If the story comes from an unfamiliar organization, check the 'about' section to learn more. Look closely at the website address. When you are reading, notice how much information there is to support the story. Genuine stories will have a lot of supporting facts. Also, look carefully at the pictures – false news stories usually contain fake images. Finally, check to see if other reliable organizations are reporting the story. If not, it may mean that the story is false. Also most important of all, use your own common sense and think critically about the stories being reported – don't believe everything you read!

Glossary

balanced (adj) considering all arguments and opinions fairly and equally
fake (adj) made to look like something real in order to trick people
genuine (adj) real rather than false
source (n) someone who provides information for a journalist

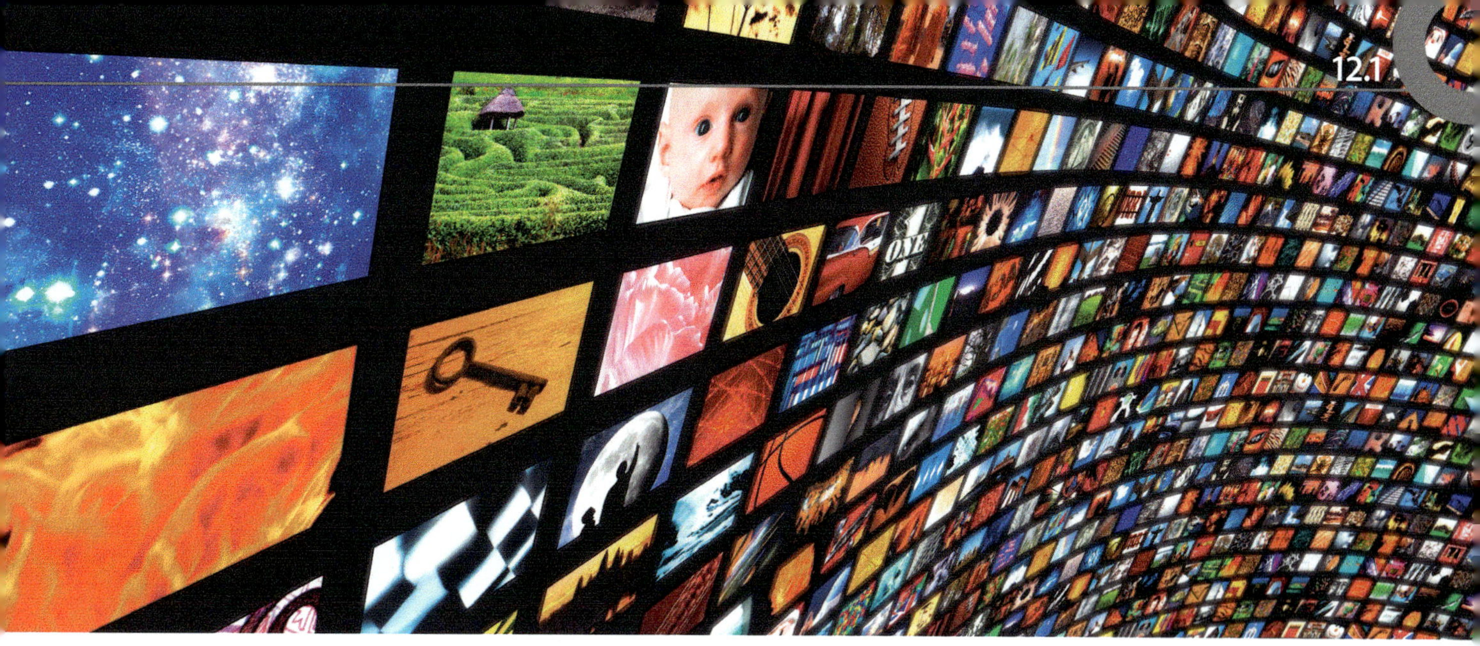

GRAMMAR

Reported speech

A **WORK IT OUT** Look at the sentences from *The news*. Do they show direct speech or are they reporting speech and ideas? What tense are the verbs in **bold**? Why is this?

*When questioned further one person said they **thought** the news **was** usually unreliable or that they **did not trust** it.*

*In contrast, those who get their news from the TV, radio or paper **said** that 'fake' or biased news **was** not really a concern.*

B Read the rules and complete the example sentences (1–4) with the correct form of the verbs.

Reported speech

When we report what people say or report their thoughts or ideas, we use a reporting verb (*said, told, asked*) and we usually change the tense of the verb(s) in the sentence (simple present → simple past, present progressive → past progressive, *will* → *would*).

- *65 percent of people said they had a preferred news website.*
- *The survey asked how often people checked the news.*
- *Most people said they would think more carefully about the news stories.*

We also do this when we report someone's words directly. We also change the pronoun (*I* → *he/she, you* → *me*)

- *'Do you like your job?'* → *She asked me if I* [1] __________ *my job.*
- *'I'm doing some work.'* → *He said he* [2] __________ *some work.*
- *'I don't think there's a lot of fake news.'* → *She said she* [3] __________ *there* [4] __________ *a lot of fake news.*
- *'I'll get back to you later.'* → *He said he* [5] __________ *back to me later.*

C Go to the **Grammar Hub** on **page XVI**.

D **SPEAK** Complete the questions with your own ideas. Then work in pairs and ask and answer each other's questions. Then work with another person and tell them what your partner's answers were.

1 What's your favorite …?

2 How often do you …?

3 Do you think you'll …?

Sara said her favorite TV show was Game of Thrones.

PRONUNCIATION

/ɒ/, /ɔː/ and /oʊ/

12.1 **A** Listen to the sounds /ɒ/, /ɔː/ and /əʊ/. They are easily confused.

1 /ɒ/ hot 2 /ɔː/ report 3 /oʊ/ hope

12.1 **B** Listen again and repeat.

12.2 **C** **SPEAK** Write the words in the correct place in the column. Be careful! One word contains two of the sounds. Listen and check.

box caught episode follow honest more online short show

/ɒ/	/ɔː/	/oʊ/

SPEAKING

A Work in groups. You are going to conduct a short survey about people's attitudes to the news. Write at least four survey questions to ask your classmates.

Where do you get most of your news?

Do you always use the same news source?

Do you think that news on the internet is generally reliable?

B Each of you interview one or two classmates and write down their answers.

C Work in groups. Discuss your findings and prepare a report of your results.

D Present your results to the class.

First, we asked where people got their news. Four people said they got it mostly from the internet, including social media. And two said they got it mostly from TV.

Talk about the pros and cons of online news

12.2 On the box

Talk and debate about different TV viewing habits

V television **G** past perfect **P** word stress in past perfect sentences

VOCABULARY
Television

A SPEAK Work in groups. Check you understand the words in **bold**. Discuss the questions.

1 Which TV **channels** do you watch the most often? What kind of **shows** do you generally watch?
2 Do you own any box sets? Do you watch on-demand TV or online streaming services?
3 Are there any **series** that you always try to watch on TV or online? How long is each **episode**? How many **seasons** of this show are there? Have there been any exciting **season finales**?

HOW BINGE-WATCHING HAS CHANGED TV FOREVER

Once upon a time
Not long ago, once a week, people regularly discussed what had happened in the previous night's episode of a certain television show. They knew that they had to wait seven long days to find out what happened next. If it was a season finale, the wait was even longer. Those days are gone.

What changed?
It all started with the DVD box set. And now, thanks to on-demand TV and internet streaming services such as Netflix (which actually started as a mail-order DVD rental service) and Amazon Prime, the way we watch television has changed forever. At the heart of this is binge-watching.

The 'now' generation
Thirty to sixty minutes of our favorite series is no longer enough. Instead, people spend hours and even whole weekends watching episode after episode. As a result, audiences are now watching more TV than ever, and around 75 percent admit to binge-watching. It is now the 'new normal'.

People want new content and they want it now. They don't want to wait to find out what happens next. Because of this, TV companies now release a complete series at one time, rather than releasing the shows episode by episode as they have done in the past.

Some of the most popular shows of all time became so successful because they could be binge-watched. As a result, a whole industry has built up around binge-watching and TV has been changed forever.

A new kind of show
Today, shows are made differently. Now, there is no need for a whole story to be contained in one episode. There is also less need for the traditional end-of-episode 'cliffhanger'. This is changing the familiar format of TV series, and show-makers now can be much more creative. For example, shows usually include actual real-world events that are happening at the same time.

TV is the new movie theater
Budgets for this new generation of TV shows are high and the shows have huge international audiences. Consequently, a lot of Hollywood stars are moving away from making traditional theater movies and appearing more on TV. At the same time, binge-watching is replacing going to the movie theater as a social occasion, with friends getting together for an evening of television. You don't actually need to be in the same physical place. Thanks to social media sites such as Twitter and Facebook, even watching alone can be a social event.

Is binge-watching here to stay?
In today's online world, people are becoming more demanding and more impatient. They want and expect everything to be immediately available. TV companies will therefore need to make more and more shows that meet this demand. As other media companies are starting to make their own TV shows, too, binge-watching will continue to be big business.

Glossary
binge-watching (n) the activity of watching TV for an extended period of time, for example, several episodes of a series
budget (n) the amount of money a person or organization has to spend on something
cliffhanger (n) an exciting end to a television show that makes you want to watch the next part
format (n) the arrangement, design or organization of something
release (v) to make a movie, TV show, etc. available for people to see or buy

READING

A Look at the title of the article and the glossary. How do you think binge-watching has changed TV? Read the article and check your answer.

B READ FOR DETAIL Read *How binge-watching has changed TV forever*. Are the sentences true (T) or false (F)? Correct the false sentences.

1 Netflix was originally a DVD manufacturer. T / F
2 We are now watching less TV than in the past. T / F
3 People binge-watch because they want to find out what happens next. T / F
4 Many shows have become successful because people could binge-watch them. T / F
5 Today, TV shows need to have a complete story in one episode. T / F
6 More and more famous movie actors are starring in TV shows. T / F

C SPEAK Work in pairs. Are you a binge-watcher? Are you addicted to TV? Go to the **Communication Hub** on **page XXIV** and take the quiz! Compare your answers.

GRAMMAR

Past perfect

A WORK IT OUT Look at the verbs in **bold** in this sentence from *How binge-watching has changed TV forever*. Which action was first, 1 or 2?

*Not long ago, once a week, people regularly [1]**discussed** what [2]**had happened** in the previous night's episode of a certain television show.*

B Choose the correct words to complete the rules.

Past perfect

1 We make the past perfect with ***had / have*** + past participle.
2 When we are talking about two events in the past, we use the past perfect to show that one event happened ***after / before*** the other.
- *I found a ticket that someone had dropped.*
- *I'd seen a couple of episodes before the one last night.*
- *I was late, but the movie hadn't started.*

3 We usually use the past perfect with *already* and *just*.
- *The bus had already left when we got to the station.*
- *The meeting had just finished when we arrived.*
- *Had you already seen the movie?*

C Go to the **Grammar Hub** on **page XVI**.

PRONUNCIATION

Word stress in past perfect sentences

12.3 **A** Listen and underline the stressed words. What happens to words that are not stressed?

1 I was late, but the movie hadn't started.
2 I found a ticket that someone had dropped.

12.3 **B** Listen and repeat.

C SPEAK Work in pairs. Underline the stressed words in the sentences. Practice saying them.

1 I'd seen a couple of episodes before the one last night.
2 The meeting had just finished when we arrived.
3 Had you already seen the movie?

D SPEAK Complete the sentences using the past perfect. Then work in groups and compare your sentences. Who has the most interesting or unusual idea for each sentence?

1 We arrived late because …
2 We didn't watch any more TV because …
3 We talked for a long time because …

SPEAKING

A Work in groups. You are going to hold a debate about which is better, box sets and on-demand viewing or more traditional weekly TV shows.

- Decide who will be in Group A and Group B.
- Group A are going to argue that box sets and on-demand viewing is better, and Group B are going to argue that more traditional weekly TV shows are better.
- Group A – go to the **Communication Hub** on **page XXII**. Group B – go to the **Communication Hub** on **page XXIII**.

B Using the ideas in the **Communication Hub** and your own ideas, plan what you are going to say and prepare your argument. Also, think about what the other group's arguments might be and prepare to argue against this.

C Hold the debate. Can you convince the other group to agree with you or to agree with some of your points?

Debating language

Building an argument
- *First, …*
- *Also, …*
- *Furthermore, …*
- *On top of that, …*

Agreeing and disagreeing
- *I (don't) agree.*
- *Yes, but …*
- *I see what you mean, but …*
- *You have a point, but …*

Talk and debate about different TV viewing habits

12.3 Advertising

Talk about advertising and what makes a good advertisement

G *should* **V** advertising **P** /æ/ and /e/ **S** identifying opinion and attitudes of speakers

LISTENING

A SPEAK Work in pairs. What do you think makes a successful advertisement?

B Look at the pictures of two different advertising campaigns. What is the product? How do you think each campaign works?

12.4 **C LISTEN FOR MAIN IDEA** Listen to two people discussing the advertising campaigns and check your answers to Exercise B.

Glossary

ad (n) an advertisement on television or radio, on the internet, in a newspaper or magazine, etc
billboard (n) a large board for advertisements in an outside public place
suck (v) to pull air or liquid somewhere

Campaign 1

Campaign 2

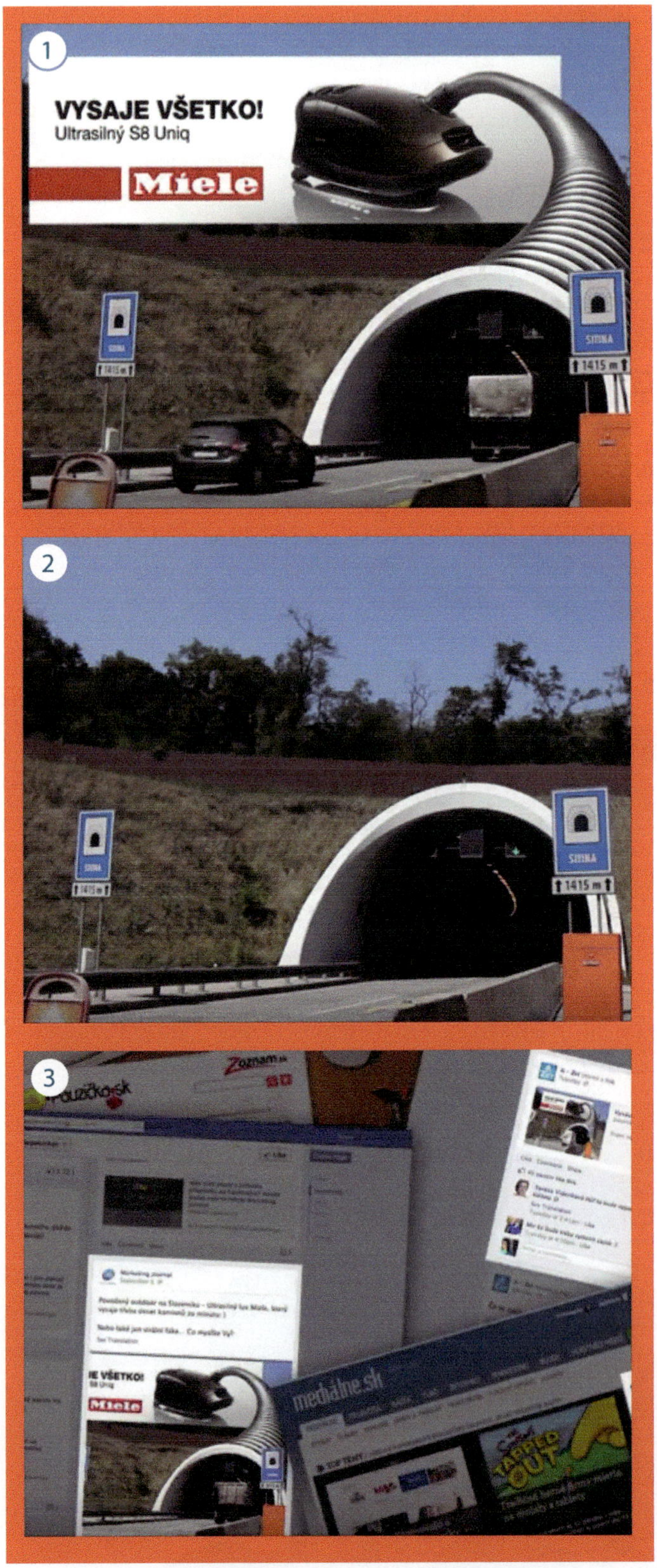

12.4 **D** Listen again. Match the sentences to *Alex*, *Kerry* or *both*. Use the information in the box to help you.

Identifying opinion and attitudes of speakers

Listen for expressions that people use to express their opinions and attitude and to agree or disagree.

Expressing opinion or attitude

I (don't) think …

In my opinion, …

… to be honest.

To agree

I agree.

Yes, … / Yes, and … / And yes, … / Yes, but …

To disagree

I don't agree. / I disagree.

Actually, …

I'm not (so) sure …

Which person (Alex, Kelly or both) think(s) …

1. the Reebok ad campaign is smart? ___
2. Alex is a fast runner? ___
3. the vacuum ad was a real billboard? ___
4. the best ads are simple and original? ___
5. an advertisement needs a clear message that you can connect with? ___
6. the most important thing about an advertisement is that you notice it? ___

E SPEAK Work in pairs. Discuss your opinion of the two ads. Which do you think is the more creative, smart or original ad? Why?

GRAMMAR

should

A Look at the sentences from the conversation between Alex and Kerry. Choose the correct words to complete the rules.

You know what, I think I might try it. ***Should*** *I?*

should

1. We usually use *should* to ***ask permission / make suggestions or offers***.
2. *Should* has ***a different meaning from / the same meaning as will***.
3. We use *should* with ***I and we / me and us***.

B Go to the **Grammar Hub** on **page XVI.**

C SPEAK Work in pairs. Make two questions with *should*. Ask and answer the questions with your partner.

VOCABULARY

Advertising

A Complete the advice about advertisements with the words in the box.

attention brand connect eye logo message slogan

What makes a good advertisement?

A good advertisement must catch your [1]___________. It needs to be original and needs to grab your [2]___________. It needs to make you stop and look at it. The image should also be something the viewer can [3]___________ with on a personal level. A good ad also needs to have a clear and simple [4]___________ and also have a catchy [5]___________, such as Nike's 'Just do it' or Microsoft's 'Where do you want to go today?' It should also have the company name or [6]___________ on the ad somewhere. But above all, the advertisement needs to tell you that the product or [7]___________ is the best there is and it needs to make you go and buy it.

B SPEAK Work in pairs. Discuss the questions.

1. How many famous logos and slogans can you think of?
2. What famous ads or advertising campaigns do you know? Do you have any favorites?

PRONUNCIATION

/æ/ and /e/

12.5 **A** Listen to the sounds /æ/ and /e/. Then underline the letters that represent /æ/ and circle the letters that represent /e/.

best brand can connect grab message

12.6 **B** Listen and check.

12.6 **C** Listen again and repeat the words.

SPEAKING HUB

A Work in groups. You are going to plan an advertising campaign for an everyday item. Go to **page XXIV** and choose the product for your campaign.

B PLAN Decide if your campaign will be an online, billboard, magazine or 'live' (like the Reebok) campaign. You may want to have a mix of these.

- Think about what makes a good advertising campaign. Consider all the points in the article *What makes a good advertisement?*
- Plan your campaign in detail. Think of a name, logo and slogan.

C PRESENT Present your advertising campaign to the class.

D REFLECT Take a class vote for the best advertising campaign.

Talk about advertising and what makes a good advertisement

Café Hub

12.4 Watch this

F– give and respond to opinions   P– agreeing and disagreeing

COMPREHENSION

A SPEAK Work in pairs. Make a list of ten different types of shows you can watch on TV. Then discuss how often you watch them.

I never watch …   I usually watch …

A: I watch dramas and movies, but I never watch documentaries. How about you?

B: I like documentaries, but most of the time I watch series.

B ▶ 00:00–01:04 Watch the first part of the video. What do Zac, Neena and Gaby want to watch?

C SPEAK Work in pairs. The roommates argue about the pros and cons of football. Predict some of the arguments.

In favor of football	Against football
	Players are paid far too much money

D ▶ 01:04–04:15 Watch the second part of the video. Do the roommates use any of your arguments in Exercise C? What do they watch in the end?

Glossary

football **(n) (British)** = soccer **(n) (American)**

MILLY

SAM

NEENA

ZAC

GABY

FUNCTIONAL LANGUAGE

Give and respond to opinions

A Write the phrases in the correct place.

I don't have a strong opinion. I'm not so sure about that. It seems to me that … That's a good idea.

Give an opinion

Personally, I think …

1 ____________________

In my view, …

Look, all I'm saying is (that) …

Agree

I completely agree!

Exactly!

Yeah, that's true.

That's fair enough.

2 ____________________

Neutral

3 ____________________

I don't mind.

Disagree

I totally disagree, I think …

Oh please! I mean, what about …

I'm sorry, Gaby, but I think …

4 ____________________

I see what you mean, but …

I see what you're saying about … but …

B Highlight the phrases that show *strong* agreement or disagreement.

PRONUNCIATION

Agreeing and disagreeing

12.7 **A** Listen to and read a conversation about agreeing and disagreeing. Then work in groups and practice the conversation copying the word stress and intonation.

Tim: Personally, I think soccer's pretty boring.

Sarah: It seems to me that soccer these days is just all about the money.

Tim: In my view, it's just some guys running around a field kicking a ball.

Beth: I completely agree.

Sarah: Exactly.

Andy: I totally disagree.

Sarah: Oh, please!

B SPEAK Work in pairs. Practice agreeing or disagreeing with each other. Talk about other professional sports, for example basketball, golf, rugby, tennis or your own ideas.

A: Personally, I think tennis players earn far too much money.

B: I see what you mean, but it's a very popular sport.

SPEAKING

A Complete the sentences with your own opinions.

1 I think ____________ is the greatest band of all time.

2 In my view, ____________ food is the best food in the world.

3 I think the safest way to travel is ____________.

4 It seems to me that most celebrities are ____________.

5 Personally, I think money makes people ____________.

B Work in pairs. Student A – read one of your sentences in Exercise A. Student B – agree or disagree. Take turns.

Give and respond to opinions

➤ Turn to page XXXI to learn how to write a story.

Unit 12 Review

VOCABULARY

A Complete the sentences with the words in the box.

breaking follow headlines report share

1 I generally ______________ the news pretty closely and check it every hour or so.

2 I always check the news ______________ as soon as I get up in the morning.

3 I have an alert on my phone that gives me any ______________ news.

4 I sometimes ______________ news stories on social media.

5 I think different news channels ______________ the news in different ways.

B Complete the crossword.

Across

4 The last episode of a season (6, 5)

5 One show in a TV series (7)

7 For example, BBC, HBO, Cartoon Network, MTV, al Jazeera (7)

8 A program that is broadcast on television or radio (4)

Down

1 A collection of DVDs or Blu-rays of the same series (3, 3)

2 You can watch at any time (2, 6)

3 A set of shows that have the same main characters or the same topic (6)

6 A set of shows as part of a series, traditionally broadcast a year before the next one (6)

C Complete the sentences with the words in the box.

attention brands connect eye logos message slogan

1 In recent years, the world's most powerful ______________ have included Lego, Google and Visa.

2 A recent survey has shown that the world's most recognizable ______________ that don't contain the company name are Nike, Apple and McDonald's.

3 A good ______________ gives a clear ______________ that people can ______________ with. One of the most successful is McDonald's 'I'm lovin' it'.

4 A good advertisement needs to catch your ______________ and grab your ______________.

GRAMMAR

A Dasha was interviewed about her attitude to online news. Read the questions and her answers. Complete what Dasha says when she reports the questions and her answers.

Q Do you have a favorite news website?

1 She asked me if *I had a favorite news website.*

A There are two or three I usually look at.

2 I said ______________

Q What kind of news stories are you interested in?

3 She asked me ______________

A I don't have a preference.

4 I said ______________

Q Are you following a news story right now?

5 She asked me ______________

A I'm following the election.

6 I told her ______________

B Complete the fact file with the verbs in parentheses. Use simple past or past perfect.

THE INVENTION OF THE TELEVISION

Before it [1]______________ (*become*) a reality, television [2]______________ (*be*) a dream of inventors for over 100 years. And by the time it was finally invented there [3]______________ (*be*) many different ideas for television. Despite the many scientists and inventors who [4]______________ (*each / play*) an important part in the development of the television, it was the British inventor John Logie Baird who on January 26, 1926 [5]______________ (*give*) the world's first demonstration of true television.

C Choose the correct words to complete the questions.

1 *Should / Will* I give you some help?

2 Who do you think *should / will* be interested in this?

3 *Should / Will* we meet at six?

4 *Should / Will* everyone understand this ad's message?

5 Who *should / will* I invite to the meeting?

FUNCTIONAL LANGUAGE

Complete the conversation with the words in the box.

disagree see seems strong true view

A: It [1]______________ to me that things are getting more and more expensive all the time.

B: Yeah, that's [2]______________. Each time I go to the grocery store, things have gone up in price.

A: In my [3]______________, soccer players' pay is disgusting!

B: I [4]______________ what you're saying, but they do give pleasure to millions of people.

A: I'm sorry, but I totally [5]______________. What do you think, Chris?

C: I don't have a [6]______________ opinion either way, to be honest. I'm not at all interested in soccer.

Endmatter Contents

Grammar Hub

Vocabulary Hub

Communication Hub

Writing

Grammar Hub

7.1 Articles

- We use *a/an* to refer to something indefinite when it is one example of many. We usually use it when we refer to something for the first time.

  *Petros told me **a** funny joke.*
- We use *the* to refer to something definite, which we know. This is usually because it has already been mentioned.

  *Petros told me a funny joke. **The** joke was about …*
- We use *the* when there is only one of something.

  *Do you usually use **the** internet?*
- We use – (no article) to refer to a plural or uncountable noun or something in a general sense.

  *I love finding **bargains** when I go shopping.*

Be careful!

- We don't use *the* before meals, days, streets, and singular place names.

  *I eat dinner at 6 every evening. NOT ~~I eat **the** dinner at 6 every evening.~~*
- We use *the* before the names of oceans and rivers and countries whose names are plural.

  ***the** Atlantic Ocean / **the** Nile River / **the** United States / **the** Philippines*
- We use *an* before a vowel sound. We use *a* before a consonant sound, even if the word begins with *a, e, i, o* or *u*.

  an article, an old friend

  a university, a European citizen

7.2 *used to*

	Positive	Negative
I/you/he/she/it/we/they	**I used to be** able to speak French.	**They didn't use to have** the internet in the 80s.

Question	Positive short answer	Negative short answer
Did you use to work hard at school?	Yes, **I did**.	No, **I didn't**.

- We use *used to* to talk about past situations that do not exist now. These include past habits and past states.

  Past habit: *We **used to watch** more TV before we had the internet.*

  Past state: *He **used to be** very anxious but he's more relaxed these days.*

Be careful!

- We use *use to* with the auxiliary verb *did*.

  *I didn't **use** to chat online for hours. NOT ~~I didn't used to chat online for hours.~~*

  *Did you **use** to be addicted to video games? NOT ~~Did you used to be addicted to video games?~~*
- In the negative, we can also say *never used to*.

  *I **didn't use** to chat online for hours. OR I **never used** to chat online for hours.*

7.3 No article (*school, the school*)

- When we are referring to a place in terms of the **activity** associated with a place, we use **no** article.

  *He studied Math in college. NOT ~~He studied Math in **the** college.~~*

  *My grandfather never went to high school. NOT ~~My grandfather never went to **the** high school.~~*
- When we are referring to the **physical place**, we use an article.

  ***The** college I go to is called Cambridge University. NOT ~~college I go to is called Cambridge University.~~ This is **a** good school. NOT ~~This is good school.~~*

7.1 Articles

A Choose the correct option.

1 The / A / – way you feel about life can affect your health.
2 I heard a great saying. *The* / *A* / – saying goes: 'Smile and the world smiles with you.'
3 George wasn't in ***the*** / ***a*** / – very good mood this morning.
4 What did you have for ***the*** / ***a*** / – lunch today?
5 *The* / *A* / – research they did into the effects of laughter was very interesting.
6 Sarah put ***the*** / ***an*** / – angry face at the end of her text message.
7 We usually have a lot of ***the*** / ***a*** / – fun at parties.

B Complete the text messages with *the*, *a*, *an* or –.

Emma: Do you want to see (**1**) ______ movie on the weekend?

Ian: Great! (**2**) ______ movie theater on Orwell Street has four screens. I'll see what's playing.

Emma: Maybe try to find (**3**) ______ comedy because (**4**) ______ horror movies and thrillers make me too scared!

Ian: Sure! I need (**5**) ______ good laugh! I'll find out and let you know.

Emma: OK. 😀

➤ Go back to page 63.

7.2 *used to*

A Correct the mistakes in each sentence.

1 I used ~~working~~ to work in a restaurant.
2 Did you used to live here?
3 They didn't used to be friends.
4 She use to study all the time.
5 We used live in Germany.
6 He used surfing the internet for hours every day.
7 You used to being good at remembering names.

B Make sentences with *used to*.

1 your school / give you / all your books / ?
Did your school use to give you all your books?
2 in the past, / people / not have / things like the internet
____
3 in the 1990s, / cell phones / be / much bigger
____
4 in the early days, / the internet / be / very unreliable
____
5 you / find / it hard / to study at school / ?
____

➤ Go back to page 65.

7.3 No article (*school, the school*)

A Complete the sentences with the words in the box. Use the definite article *the* if necessary.

college ~~college~~ prison school school

1 I started studying math in ___college___ but I soon dropped out.
2 They brought the child up badly and he ended up in _______________ for robbery.
3 The _______________ next to my house is called Gregory's. It's for talented children.
4 It's easy to make friends at _______________. I had lots as a kid.
5 Anna also went to _______________ where I studied Law.

B Complete the text with *the* or – (no article).

(1) ___The___ college I work at is called St. Anne's. I'm a professor there. When I was a kid, I used to hate (2) _________ school. (3) _________ school I went to was very bad and it didn't have good amenities. I loved it when I went to (4) _________ college, though, because (5) _________ college I studied at was very modern, and it's also where I met my best friend, Jillian.

➤ Go back to page 67.

Grammar Hub

8.1 Reflexive pronouns

Subject pronoun	Reflexive pronoun	
I	myself	I see **myself** performing in this band for two more years.
you (singular)	yourself	You know **yourself** better than anyone else does.
him	himself	He works for **himself** as a photographer.
her	herself	She's the only actress I know who likes watching **herself** on TV.
it	itself	This problem won't fix **itself**. We need to do something.
we	ourselves	We are going to treat **ourselves** to front row seats at the theater.
you (plural)	yourselves	I hope you all enjoyed **yourselves** at the show.
they	themselves	They bought **themselves** an expensive sculpture.

- We use a reflexive pronoun as the object of a verb when the subject and the object are the same person or thing.

  I taught ***myself*** *how to play the guitar.*
- We can use a reflexive pronoun after the object of a verb. This is to emphasise the person or thing that does the action.

  She chose the costumes for the play ***herself****.*
- We use *by* + reflexive pronoun to say we do something alone or with no help.

  He worked out what had happened ***by himself****.*
- For emphasis, we can also use *all by* + reflexive pronoun.

  I can't believe you did it ***all by*** *yourself!*
- We use *each other* when two or more people or things perform the same action to the other person/people.

  Eric and Patricia sang ***each other*** *a song.* NOT ~~*Eric and Patricia sang* ***themselves*** *a song.*~~

Be careful!

- We don't use reflexive pronouns after prepositions of place. We use object pronouns.

  I took my camera with ***me****.* NOT ~~*I took my camera with* ***myself****.*~~

8.2 Infinitive of purpose

- We can use *to* + base form when we express the purpose or reason for doing something.

  I went to the art store ***to get*** *some paint.*

  We went to the ticket office early ***to avoid*** *the lines.*

Be careful!

Trine went to the concert ***to see*** *her favorite band perform.* NOT ~~*Trine went to the concert* ***seeing*** *her favorite band perform.*~~

8.3 First conditional

Condition *If* + simple present,	Result *will/won't*
If **you go** to the festival,	**you'll have** a great time.
If **it doesn't rain**,	**we'll go** to the street fair.
If **it's** busy,	**we won't go** to the theater.
If **you don't ask** for help,	**you won't get** any.

Result *will/won't*	Condition *if* + simple present
You'll meet the artist	if **you visit** the gallery tonight.
She won't go to the concert	if **it's** expensive.

Question	Positive short answer	Negative short answer
If Star Wars **is** playing at the movie theater, **will you go**?	Yes, **I will**.	No, **I won't**.
Will you go if Star Wars **is** playing at the movie theater?		

- We use the first conditional to talk about possible situations in the future.
- The *if*-clause describes the action or condition.

  If he sells all his art*, he'll get a bigger studio.*

  The result clause says what will happen.

  If he sells all his art, ***he'll get a bigger studio****.*
- We can use other modal verbs (e.g. *can, could, might, should*) instead of *will*.

  If you sing really well, you ***can*** *become famous.*

  If it's open, we ***might*** *go to the museum.*

  If you win an award, we ***should*** *celebrate.*
- We can use *should* to ask questions and make suggestions.

  Should *we work on our paintings if you're not too tired?*

Be careful!

- We use a comma (,) when the *if*-clause comes first.

  If you go, I'll come too. NOT ~~*If you go I'll come too.*~~

  I'll buy your ticket if you get the popcorn. NOT ~~*I'll buy your ticket, if you get the popcorn.*~~

8.1 Reflexive pronouns

A Correct the mistakes in each sentence.

1 I bought ~~me~~ *myself* a membership to a book club.
2 We didn't give ourself enough time to set up the exhibit.
3 Paul, be careful! Please don't hurt himself climbing over those seats.
4 He wrote the songs for his album all by itself.
5 You look tired, Eleni. You should look after yourselves and get more sleep.
6 I wish our friends Pete and Lynne could be ourselves around strangers.
7 The show I organized ran myself – it didn't take a lot of work.

B Write the missing reflexive pronoun.

1 We bought *ourselves* a new piano.
2 Jane, please don't compare ______ to other people.
3 Rachel hurt ______ singing on stage.
4 The problem with my music player fixed ______.
5 They bought ______ tickets to see Adele in concert.
6 He asked ______ if he was happy as a writer.
7 We must learn to love ______ before we can love others.

➤ Go back to page 73.

8.2 Infinitive of purpose

A Make sentences with *to* + base form.

1 I / play / the violin / relax
I play the violin to relax.
2 she / attend / drawing classes / spend / time / with other artists
______
3 we / go / to the movie theater / early / get / good seats
______
4 some people / visit / Paris / just / see / the Louvre
______
5 they / sell / their art / on the street / last weekend / make / money
______
6 she / go / to voice lessons / every evening / improve / her singing
______
7 we / travel / to Florence / next year / do / some photography
______

➤ Go back to page 75.

8.3 First conditional

A Check (✓) the sentences that are correct. Correct the mistakes in the others.

1 She will give you an autograph if you ~~will~~ ask her.
2 If I have time, I will paint your portrait tomorrow. ✓
3 He stars in the movie if they pay him well.
4 I go with you to the movie theater if we can watch a comedy.
5 The audience will love us, if we play our best songs.
6 If we all join the book club, it will be a lot of fun.

B Complete the sentences with the correct form of the verbs in the box.

ask buy ~~call~~ go have like

1 I *'ll call* Claire if you call Simon.
2 If you get the movie tickets, I ______ the snacks.
3 If it rains tomorrow, we ______ a concert in the park.
4 I ______ to the audition if you come with me.
5 You'll love *Wicked* if you ______ musicals.
6 If she ______ for my help, I'll give it to her.

C Complete the conversation with the correct form of the verbs in parentheses.

Wes: (1) What about next week's gallery opening? If you *organize* (*organize*) the food, I *'ll take care of* (*take care of*) the drinks.
Trisha: (2) OK. What about setting up the artwork? If I ______ (*do*) that, ______ (*you / send*) out the invitations?
Wes: (3) Sure. Should I invite students from the university? If they ______ (*come*), we ______ (*not have*) enough food and drinks.
Trisha: (4) I know … It's a problem. If we ______ (*invite*) all of them, the gallery ______ (*get*) too full!
Wes: (5) If everyone ______ (*show*) up, there ______ (*probably / not be*) enough space.
Trisha: (6) If that ______ (*happen*), people ______ (*might damage*) the art.
Wes: You're right. Let's not invite them, then.

➤ Go back to page 77.

Grammar Hub

9.1 Second conditional

Condition *If + simple past,*	Result *would/wouldn't*
If **you spent** less money,	**you would be** happier.
If **I didn't work** all the time,	**I'd make** more friends.
If **it were** expensive,	**I wouldn't buy** it.
If **they didn't travel** a lot,	**they wouldn't gain** new experiences.

Result *would/wouldn't*	Condition *if + simple past*
You'd discover your interests	if **you traveled** more.
She wouldn't do it	if **she didn't want** to.

Question	Positive short answer	Negative short answer
If **you had** a lot of money, **would you give** it to charity?	Yes, **I would**.	No, **I wouldn't**.
Would you give money to charity if **you had** a lot?		

- We use the second conditional to talk about hypothetical situations in the present or future. The *if*-clauses can be an unlikely or impossible situation.

  Unlikely: *If I **won** the London marathon, I **would be** so happy!*

  Impossible: *If I **were** you, I **wouldn't lend** him the money.*
- We only use a comma (,) when the *if*-clause comes first.
- We can use other modal verbs (e.g. *could*, *might*) as an alternative to *would* in the main clause.

  *If she tried something new, it **could open** her mind.*
  *If you had more free time, you **might feel** happier.*
- When the *if*-clause is clear or is implied, we usually only state the result clause.

  What would you do if you won a million dollars?
  I'd leave my job! And I might buy a new house.

Be careful!

- With *I*, *he*, *she* and *it*, we usually use *were* in the *if*-clause, not *was*.

  *If I **were** rich, I would give money to my favorite charity.*
- We only use *would* in the result clause.

  If we had children, we'd buy a bigger house. NOT ~~*If we would have a family, we'd buy a bigger house.*~~

9.2 Essential adjective clauses

	Relative pronoun	
Person	who	The friend **who** lent me the money is named Jack.
	that	The person **that** gave away the money is a billionaire.
Thing	which	The salary **which** I earn is too small.
	that	The donation **that** he made is very large.
Possession	whose	The man **whose** wallet I found thanked me.
Place	where	The company **where** I work supports many charities.
Time	when	The year **when** Rockefeller died was 1937.

- We use an essential adjective clause to give information about and identify a noun (person or thing).
- We can use *who* or *that* for people, and *which* or *that* for things.

  *The person **who** lent me the money is named Jack.* OR *The person **that** lent me the money is named Jack.*
  *The donation **that** he made is very large.* OR *The donation **which** he made is very large.*
- We can leave out the relative pronoun when it is followed by a subject and verb, rather than just a verb.

  Relative pronoun + subject and verb: *The charity **that** she supports helps animals.* OR *The charity she supports helps animals.*

  Relative pronoun + verb: *The person **that lent** me the money is named Jack.* NOT ~~*The person **lent** me the money is named Jack.*~~

9.3 Gerunds

- Gerunds are a type of noun.

  Noun: *He likes **clothes**.*
  Gerund: *He likes **shopping**.*
  Noun: ***Money** doesn't bring happiness.*
  Gerund: ***Owning** things doesn't bring happiness.*
- We use gerunds after prepositions.

  *I dream **about setting up** my own business.*
  *He's good **at trading** things online.*
- We can use gerunds directly after some verbs. See Grammar Reference 3.3 for more information.

  *They **like** making a profit.*
  *We **love** doing online research.*
- We can use gerunds as either subjects or objects.

  *Subject: **Cleaning** the house is boring.*
  *Object: She hates **cleaning** the house.*
- Gerunds can act like verbs and take an object.

  *She hates doing **the ironing**.*

Be careful!

- If the verb ends in *-e*, remove the final *-e* before adding *-ing*.

  make → making — *He enjoys **making** money.*
  give → giving — *She likes **giving** money to charity.*

9.1 Second conditional

A Correct the mistakes in each sentence. Make second conditionals.

1 If I could travel, I would discover more about myself.
2 If people aren't obsessed with money, the world would be a better place.
3 If I had the choice, I will buy experiences, not possessions.
4 Carol would travel more if she have not children.
5 You would inspire other people if you would do something amazing.
6 Did you throw away your all possessions if I asked you?
7 If I could take two months off work, I traveled around India.

B Complete the conversation with the correct form of the verbs in parentheses.

Molly: I just played the lotto. It's $10 million tonight. Imagine what (**1**) would happen (*happen*) if I (**2**) ________ (*win*)!

Nelly: Well, you (**3**) ________ (*be*) rich – that's for sure! What (**4**) ________ (*you / do*) with the money?

Molly: If I (**5**) ________ (*have*) $10 million, I (**6**) ________ (*give*) most of it to my family, or to charity, you know?

Nelly: Really? I (**7**) ________ (*not / do*) that. I'd buy a big house, and some expensive artwork.

➤ Go back to page 83.

9.2 Essential adjective clauses

A Choose the correct option.

1 I know many people *which* / *who* would love to travel.
2 The student *who* / *whose* father is a well-known philanthropist has plenty of money.
3 The charity *who* / *that* I usually donate to is *Help the Children*.
4 This is the city *where* / *which* I went to college.
5 Wealthy people *that* / *which* join the Giving Pledge can inspire others.
6 That was the time *when* / *where* Rockefeller gave away most of his fortune.
7 He started his own charity *which* / *whose* helps protect the environment.

B Match to make sentences.

1 My cell phone is the possession b
2 The London Marathon is an event ___
3 Andrew Carnegie was another person who ___
4 The money ___
5 She's the woman ___
6 South America is where ___
7 She gained a lot of experience ___

a gave away most of his wealth.
b that I could never give away!
c she traveled as a student.
d that raises millions of dollars for charity.
e that he left will be given to charity.
f when she was traveling in India.
g who set up the charity.

➤ Go back to page 85.

9.3 Gerunds

A Complete the sentences with the gerund form of the verbs in the box.

do give have make ~~save~~ set up spend

1 He isn't very good at saving money.
2 She usually dreams of ________ a family of her own.
3 Gareth is looking forward to ________ his own business.
4 Andrew Carnegie was famous for ________ away almost all his money.
5 ________ research is one of the most enjoyable things about my course.
6 We really need to stop ________ so much money on entertainment.
7 We hope that our business will start ________ a profit.

B Complete the sentences with the gerund form of the verb in parentheses. Then choose subject gerund (*S*) or object gerund (*O*).

1 They aren't good at making (*make*) a living. *S* / *O*
2 ________ (*dream*) of new places to visit is my favorite way to pass the time. *S* / *O*
3 ________ (*spend*) money on designer clothing is a total waste. *S* / *O*
4 The most important thing to practice and be good at is ________ (*be*) yourself. *S* / *O*
5 Saving money may involve ________ (*do*) without certain luxuries. *S* / *O*
6 ________ (*be*) a successful trader is harder than it sounds. *S* / *O*
7 You cannot enjoy life unless you spend it ________ (*live*) for today. *S* / *O*

➤ Go back to page 87.

Grammar Hub

10.1 Comparatives and superlatives

	Comparative	Superlative
One syllable adjective	adj + *-er* (+ *than*) slow → slow**er**	*the* + adj + *-est* cheap → **the** cheap**est**
Short adjectives ending in *-e*	adj + *-r* (+ *than*) late → late**r**	*the* + adj + *-st* late → **the** late**st**
Short adjectives ending in one vowel + one consonant	double the consonant + *-er* (+ *than*) big → big**ger**	*the* + double the consonant + *-est* big → **the** big**gest**
Adjectives ending in *-y*	adj without *-y* + *-ier* (+ *than*) easy → eas**ier**	*the* + adj without *-y* + *-iest* heavy → **the** heav**iest**
Longer adjectives (two + syllables)	*more* + adj (+ *than*) expensive → **more** expensive	the most + adj useful → **the most** useful
Irregular adjectives	good → **better**	good → **the best**
Regular adverbs	*more* + adv (+ *than*) quickly → **more** quickly	the most + adv efficiently→ **the most** efficiently
Irregular adverbs	badly → worse far → farther/further fast → faster hard → harder well → better	badly → the worst far → the farthest/furthest fast → the fastest hard → the hardest well → the best

- We use comparatives to say how two or more things are different.
- We use superlatives to say that something is top or bottom of a group.
- To make a negative comparative, we use *less* instead of *more*.

  *My e-reader was **less** expensive than yours.*
- To make a negative superlative, we use *the least* instead of *the most*.

  *This phone works **the least** efficiently of them all.*
- We use the pattern *get/become* + comparative adjective + *and* + the same comparative adjective to talk about change over time.

  *Computers are **getting smaller and smaller**.*
- For longer adjectives, we use *get/become* + *more and more* + comparative adjective.

  *Computer games are **becoming more and more realistic**.*

Be careful!

- We only use *than* when it is followed by the thing we are comparing.

  This phone is better than this phone.
  NOT ~~This phone is good but this one is better than.~~
- We don't put *the* before a superlative when we use a possessive adjective.

  What was your biggest mistake when buying gadgets? NOT ~~What was your the biggest mistake when buying gadgets?~~

10.2 More comparative structures

- We use *as* + adjective/adverb + *as* to say that two things are the same in some way.

  *Your phone is **as good as** mine.*
  *My drone flies **as quickly as** yours.*
- For emphasis, we use *just as … as*.

  *You are **just as** good **as** I am at this video game.*
- We use *not as* + adjective/adverb + *as* to say that two things are different in some way.

  *Your computer **isn't as fast as** mine.*
  *I **don't** use technology **as regularly as** you do.*

10.3 *need to*

	Positive	Negative
I/you/we/they	**You need to prove** what you're saying.	**We don't need to do** any more research.
he/she/it	**He needs to make** preparations.	**She doesn't need to wear** a spacesuit.

Question	Positive short answer	Negative short answer
Do you need to prepare for the test?	Yes, **I do**.	No, **I don't**.
Does she need to report her findings?	Yes, **she does**.	No, **she doesn't**.

- We use *need to* like *have to* to say that something is or isn't necessary.

  *Astronauts **need to** be fit. OR Astronauts **have to** be fit.*
  *Astronauts **don't need** to be young. OR Astronauts **don't have to** be young.*
- The verb *need* is followed by *to* + infinitive.

  *Astronauts need **to be** fit. NOT ~~Astronauts need being fit.~~*

10.1 Comparatives and superlatives

A Correct the mistakes in each sentence.

1 Exercising is a lot more ~~interested~~ *interesting* with a fitness tracker.
2 This is the better device I've ever owned.
3 You bought the more expensive phone in the store.
4 This laptop is worst than my old one.
5 Your tablet is more light than mine.
6 This tablet starts the more quickly than my other devices.
7 Technology is getting more the more advanced.

B Complete the sentences with the correct form of the adjectives and adverbs in parentheses.

1 This new cell phone is *lighter* (*light*) than my old one.
2 My computer is ______________ (*expensive*) thing I own.
3 An e-reader is ______________ (*good*) for reading books than a laptop.
4 Computers are getting ______________ and ______________ (*cheap*) every year.
5 You can check spelling ______________ (*quick*) online than you can by using a dictionary.
6 Although my phone was ______________ (*heavy*) one in the store, I bought it for all its features.

➤ Go back to page 93.

10.2 More comparative structures

A Choose the correct option.

1 When my computer crashes, I get *just* / (*as*) annoyed as everyone else does.
2 My tablet is ***as not*** / ***not as*** useful as I thought it would be.
3 Is your drone ***as much fun*** / ***fun as much*** as you expected it to be?
4 Getting more computer memory is ***just as simple as*** / ***simple as just*** connecting a USB.
5 Video calls are as cheap ***than*** / ***as*** normal calls on a computer.
6 This GPS is not ***as reliable as*** / ***reliable as*** it should be.
7 Your internet connection is just ***as fast as*** / ***fast as*** mine.

B Make sentences. Use contractions where possible.

1 tablets … = useful … laptops
Tablets are just as useful as laptops.
2 tablets … > useful … laptops
Laptops aren't as useful as tablets.
3 TV advertising … > effective … advertising on the radio
____
4 the GPS on my phone … = good … the GPS in the car
____
5 4G … > fast … 3G internet
____
6 new models … > reliable … old models
____

➤ Go back to page 95.

10.3 *need to*

A Make questions with *need to*. Then write short answers.

1 you / need / find / a solution ✓
Do you need to find a solution? Yes, I/we do.
2 astronauts / need / wear / spacesuits all the time ✗
____
3 she / need / follow / a schedule ✗
____
4 the food / need / be / canned ✓
____
5 astronauts / need / be / fit ✓
____
6 I / need / repair / this computer ✗
____

B Make sentences with *need to*.

1 You / not / use a telescope to see the ISS
You don't need to use a telescope to see the ISS.
2 the scientists / do / more research on the subject
____
3 people / think / about the future
____
4 you / find / a solution
____
5 he / confirm / what he believes
____
6 they / not / install / an app
____

➤ Go back to page 97.

Grammar Hub

11.1 The passive voice (simple present and simple past)

	Positive	Negative
I	**I am told** the desert is beautiful.	**I'm not expected** to be an expert on the environment.
he/she/it	It **is visited** by lots of people.	**It is not understood** by many people. **It isn't understood** by many people.
you/we/they	**You are advised** to stay away from the volcano.	**They aren't studied** by scientists.

Question	Positive short answer	Negative short answer
Am I allowed to take photographs?	Yes, **you are**.	No, **you aren't**.
Are we permitted to get close to the waterfall?	Yes, **we/you are**.	No, **we/you aren't**.

	Positive	Negative
I/he/she/it	**I was told** to read the article.	**She wasn't asked** to help.
you/we/they	They **were invited** to the island.	The clothes **weren't needed** on the journey.

Question	Positive short answer	Negative short answer
Was she joined by her friends?	Yes, **she was**.	No, **she wasn't**.
Were they told what to do?	Yes, **they were**.	No, **they weren't**.

- We use the passive voice when we don't say who or what causes the action (usually because the person or thing is not known, not important or obvious).

  *The new road to the site **was opened** last year.*
- We also use the passive voice with *by* when we know who does/did an action and we want to emphasize it.

  *This report was produced **by** scientists from Cambridge University.*
- We can sometimes say the same thing in the active or passive voice. The choice usually depends on the topic we are talking about.

  Active: *Many tourists **visit** the site.* (The topic is tourists.)

  Passive: *The site **is visited** by many tourists.* (The topic is the site.)

Be careful!

- We don't use *by* + the agent unless it is important, useful information.

  The research is paid for by the World Wildlife Fund. NOT ~~*The research is paid for by someone.*~~

11.2 Adjective + infinitive

- When we want to use an adjective to describe an action, we can use adjective + infinitive.

  *It's **interesting to study** the life cycle of a mammal.*

  *It was **nice to watch** animals in their natural habitat.*
- When we want to say that an adjective doesn't describe an action, we use the negative form of the verb.

  *It **wasn't** easy to make a living as a scientist.*
- When we want to say that an adjective describes the opposite of an action, we use *not* + infinitive.

  *It's important **not to do** any damage to the environment.*

11.3 *even*

- We use *even* as an adverb to suggest that something is surprising.

  *Recycling is not difficult – there is **even** a recycling bin at the office.*

  *You don't **even** have to leave your room to find things made of plastic.*

  *She doesn't **even** know where the Pacific Ocean is!*
- We use *even* before main verbs and after auxiliary verbs and modals.

  *We **even found** plastic waste on Mount Everest.*

  NOT ~~*We found even plastic waste on Mount Everest.*~~

  *Plastic **can even** be found on Mars* NOT ~~*Plastic even can be found on Mars.*~~
- We can also use *even* before nouns.

  ***Even** experts make mistakes sometimes.*

11.1 The passive voice (simple present and simple past)

A Correct the mistakes in each sentence.

1 The volcano ^is located in the middle of a jungle.
2 The cliffs were form 200 million years ago.
3 The museum opened by the President last night.
4 The mountain is make of a strong type of rock.
5 The city doesn't known for its art.
6 The new park wasn't open by anyone famous.
7 She attracted to Africa because of the wildlife.

B Complete the text messages with the correct passive form of the verbs in parentheses.

Gloria: How was your trip to Uluru?

Toby: Great! I learned a lot. I (**1**) was helped (*help*) by all the tourist information there.

Gloria: Like what?

Toby: Well, it (**2**) ________ (*make*) of sandstone and it's nearly 350m high.

Gloria: Cool. What else did you learn?

Toby: It (**3**) ________ (*create*) over 600 million years ago.

Gloria: Wow, that's really old!

Toby: I know! Also, it (**4**) ________ (*own*) by the native Australian people.

Gloria: I thought the government owned it.

Toby: It's (**5**) ________ (*not own*) by them. They just manage it.

➤ Go back to page 103.

11.2 Adjective + infinitive

A Put the words in order to make sentences.

1 easy / understand / a person's / it's / to / body language
It's easy to understand a person's body language.
2 necessary / be / it's / quiet / to / near / wild animals
____
3 fascinating / take / was / photos of insects / to / it
____
4 good / live / green / a / it's / to / lifestyle
____
5 to / is / educational / it / wildlife shows / watch / ?
____

B Choose the correct option.

1 It's *good not* / *not good* to feed the animals in the zoo.
2 It's *important not* / *not important* to make wild animals angry or upset.
3 It's *not easy* / *easy not* to take the perfect photo.
4 It's *necessary not* / *not necessary* to be an expert to enjoy studying animals.
5 It's *not essential* / *essential not* to go near crocodiles.
6 It's *not safe* / *safe not* to go traveling in the wild on your own.
7 It's *essential not* / *not essential* to have top quality equipment in order to take great photos.

➤ Go back to page 105.

11.3 *even*

A Choose the correct place to put *even*, A or B.

1 Most (A) people haven't (B) thought about it before.
2 (A) some experts are surprised (B) that the problem is so serious.
3 A lot of people (A) don't (B) realize that plastic lasts so long.
4 There (A) is (B) a place to recycle glass on my street.
5 You (A) can't (B) walk 100 meters without seeing some plastic that has been thrown away.

B Put *even* in the correct place in each sentence.

1 A lot of people don't ^even notice the pollution.
2 The base camp for Mount Aconcagua is very high.
3 There are many solutions – we can stop using plastic.
4 There are a lot of organizations in my town – there's a bird-watchers' club.
5 I love all animals, and I like spiders.
6 I know some adults who don't know the difference between a lion and a tiger.

➤ Go back to page 107.

Grammar Hub

12.1 Reported speech

Direct speech	Reported speech
simple present '**We like** Channel 4 News best.' '**Do you like** Channel 4 News best?'	simple past Most people said (that) **they liked** Channel 4 News best. She asked them if **they liked** Channel 4 News best.
present progressive '**We are watching** the news.'	past progressive They said (that) **they were watching** the news.
will '**I will** watch TV later.'	*would* She said (that) **she would** watch TV later.
may '**Elle may** buy the box set.'	*might* He said (that) **Elle might** buy the box set.
can '**We can** record the episode.'	*could* They said (that) **they could** record the episode.

- We use reported speech to report what people say or report their thoughts or ideas.
- We use a reporting verb in the simple past.

  *He **said** … They **told** me … She **asked** him if …*
- We usually go back one tense from the tense the speaker used, but we usually don't go back one tense with the simple past.

  *'I'**m watching** TV.' → He said he **was watching** TV.*
  *'We usually **went** to the movie theater.' → He said they usually **went** to the movie theater.*
- We also need to change some pronouns (*I* to *he/she*, *my* to *his/her*, *your* to *my*, etc).

  *'I like **your** radio show,' said Lola. →*
  *Lola told me that **she** liked **my** radio show.*
- We sometimes also need to change other words.

Direct speech	Reported speech
now 'We're going to watch the news **now**.'	*then / right now* They said they were going to watch the news **then / right now**.
tonight 'I will be on social media **tonight**.'	*that night* He said he would be on social media **that night**.
tomorrow 'We'll set the budget **tomorrow**.'	*the next day / the following day* She said they would set the budget **the next day**.
today 'That new show is on TV **today**.'	*that day* He said that new show was on TV **that day**.
here 'There are some reporters **here**.'	*there* She said there were some reporters **there**.

12.2 Past perfect

	Positive	Negative
I/you/he/she/it/we/they	**I'd heard** the story before you read it.	**She hadn't seen** the ad before yesterday.

Question	Positive short answer	Negative short answer
Had you visited the news website before?	Yes, **I had**.	No, **I hadn't**.

- When we are talking about two events in the past, we use the past perfect to show that one event happened before the other.

  past ————————→ present
  ↑ I saw you on the news. ↑ You told me about it.

  *I **had seen** you on the news before you told me about it.*
- We usually use *just* and *already* with the past perfect.

  *The movie had **just** started when we arrived at the movie theater.*
  *Had they seen the show **already**?*

Be careful!

- If we use the simple past with *when*, the meaning is different to when we use the past perfect.

  *I **checked the news** when I left. (= I checked the news **after** I left.)*
  *I **had checked the news** when I left. (= I checked the news **before** I left.)*

12.3 *should*

Subject	Question
I/we	**Should I buy** tickets for the movie?

- We use *should* to make offers and suggestions.

  offer: *Should **I turn** the TV on?*
  suggestion: ***Should we** go to the movie theater tonight?*
- We also use *should* to ask for suggestions.

  *Which episode **should we watch** this evening?*

Be careful!

- We only use *should* with *I* and *we*.

  *Which episode **should we watch** this evening?* NOT ~~*Which episode should you watch this evening?*~~

- We use *will* to ask questions about the future.

  ***Will you binge-watch** the show this weekend?*

12.1 Reported speech

A Report the statements.

1 Paul and James: 'We're going shopping tonight.'
They said *(that) they were going shopping that night.*

2 Tina: 'I'll post it online later.'
She said ______

3 Roy: 'I can't help with the budget.'
He said ______

4 James: 'Don't watch the show without me!'
He told me ______

5 Helen: 'Can I borrow your box set?'
She asked me if ______

6 Alan: 'Are they going to show the ad tonight?'
He asked me if ______

7 Nora: 'You may need to speak to a journalist today.'
She told me that ______

B Complete the text messages with the correct form of the verbs in parentheses.

Pat: Fred said you (**1**) *went* (*go*) to the movie theater with him the other night.

Nuala: Yeah. He told me he (**2**) ______ (*want*) to watch a new sci-fi movie, but I asked him if we (**3**) ______ (*can*) see a comedy instead. I said I (**4**) ______ (*not feel*) like seeing a serious movie.

Pat: He said you (**5**) ______ (*see*) *Ride Away* in the end. Was it good?

Nuala: That's right. We (**6**) ______ (*be going to*) choose *Hideout*, but it was on too late. *Ride Away* was the best option.

➤ Go back to page 113.

12.2 Past perfect

A Correct the mistakes in each sentence.

1 Someone had ~~drop~~ *dropped* a newspaper on the ground.

2 I was late, but the movie wasn't starting, so it was OK.

3 The show have just begun when we arrived.

4 They had saw the movie twice already.

5 The journalist has already left when she got to the meeting.

6 Had you just seen the show before last night?

7 **A:** Had she posted it before?
B: Yes, she did.

B Complete each sentence with the correct form of the verb in parentheses.

1 The movie *had already begun* (*already begin*) when I arrived.

2 I didn't watch the movie because I ______ (*already see*) it.

3 They didn't want to watch the news because they ______ (*already read*) the newspaper.

4 We ______ (*just start*) the trip home when the accident happened.

5 I ______ (*find*) the DVD that my girlfriend had dropped behind the couch.

➤ Go back to page 115.

12.3 *should*

A Choose the correct option.

1 *Should* (circled) / *Will* we see what's on TV?

2 *Should* / *Will* I invite Amy over to watch the show?

3 *Should* / *Will* they release the show on DVD soon?

4 *Should* / *Will* we binge-watch the show this weekend?

5 *Should* / *Will* this catch people's attention?

6 What movie *should* / *will* we see at the movie theater?

7 What *should* / *will* you say to the journalist?

B Write questions using *should* or *will*.

1 we / share / our photos online tonight
Should we share our photos online tonight?

2 they / release / the new movie / this weekend
______

3 I / pay / for the movie tickets
______

4 she / finish / her journalism course this year
______

5 we / watch / something exciting this weekend
______

➤ Go back to page 117.

Vocabulary Hub

7.1 Feelings

A Match the adjectives (1–6) with their meanings (a–f).

1 pleased
2 cheerful
3 confused
4 anxious
5 relaxed
6 scared

a frightened or worried
b calm and not worried
c worried because you think something bad might happen
d happy and satisfied
e behaving in a happy, friendly way
f unable to understand something or think clearly about it

B Which words in Exercise A have similar meanings to these words? Are the words positive or negative?

glad: ______________, ______________

nervous: ______________, ______________

C Complete the sentences with adjectives from Exercise A. More than one answer may be possible.

1 I'm feeling ______________ because I have an exam tomorrow.
2 Olaf's finished all of his work, so he's in a ______________ mood.
3 That was a hard day, but now it's over I can feel ______________ .
4 I'm not going anywhere near that spider – I'm too ______________ .
5 I don't understand these questions – they just make me feel ______________ .
6 Jordi's really ______________ now that he has passed his driving test.

➤ Go back to page 63.

7.2 Shortened words

A Work in pairs. How do you shorten these words? Circle the parts of the words that can be shortened.

internet
introduction
website
information
laboratory
newspaper
airplane
suitcase
cell phone
microphone

B Complete the sentences with shortened words from Exercise A.

1 We need more ______________ before we can make a final decision.
2 The singer dropped the ______________ halfway through the song.
3 So many of the ______________ on the ______________ are basically just full of pictures of people's cats.
4 I asked the staff to let me take my ______________ on to the ______________ as carry-on luggage.
5 Read the ______________ to this article in the ______________ and see if you can understand it.
6 My parents are going to buy me a new ______________ when I start working in the ______________ at college.

➤ Go back to page 65.

8.1 Music

Label the pictures (1–2) with the words in the box. You will need to use some words more than once.

audience drummer drums guitar
guitarist keyboard player keyboards
light show microphone singer stage

1

2

8.2 Types of art

Look at the pictures (1–8). Label them with the words in the box.

abstract art   exhibit   gallery   landscape
photograph   portrait   sculpture   still life

The Hay Wain by John Constable

1 ______________

Sunflowers by Vincent van Gogh

2 ______________

Mona Lisa by Leonardo da Vinci

3 ______________

Guitar on a Chair by Juan Gris

4 ______________

David by Michelangelo

5 ______________

Lunch atop a Skyscraper by Charles C Ebbets

6 ______________

A collection of landscapes

7 ______________

The Louvre, Paris

8 ______________

➤ Go back to page 74.

9.3 *make* and *do* expressions

Match the expressions (1–6) with the pictures (a–f).

1 make a mess   **2** make a mistake   **3** do some damage
4 make a decision   **5** do your homework   **6** make a complaint

a

b

c

d

e

f

➤ Go back to page 87.

10.1 Electronic devices

A Label the pictures of electronic devices (1–6) with the words in the box.

drone e-reader fitness tracker
power bank tablet USB drive

1 ______________

2 ______________

3 ______________

4 ______________

5 ______________

6 ______________

B Complete the sentences with the devices in Exercise A. There is one word you do not need.

1 A ______________ is great when you are not at home and your phone battery runs out.

2 He always uses his ______________ to transfer large files.

3 I wear my ______________ 24 hours a day. I love it because it tells me how many steps I take.

4 Tina got a ______________ for her birthday, but she was flying it in the backyard and it got stuck up in a tree!

5 My husband won't buy an ______________ because he says he loves the feel and smell of paper books.

➤ Go back to page 92.

11.1 Natural features

Label the pictures (1–8) with the words in the box.

bay canal cave cliff desert ocean rainforest valley

1 ______________

2 ______________

3 ______________

4 ______________

5 ______________

6 ______________

7 ______________

8 ______________

➤ Go back to page 102.

11.2 Animals

Write the animal words in the box in the correct place.

alligator ant ~~bear~~ bee butterfly crocodile duck
eagle elephant fly frog gorilla lion lizard
monkey mosquito moth owl panda parrot
penguin shark snake tiger toad tuna

Mammals	Birds	Insects
bear		

Reptiles	Amphibians	Fish

➤ Go back to page 104.

7.3 Student A

MICHAEL KEARNEY:
the world's youngest college graduate

1984: born and grew up in Honolulu, Hawaii

4 months: spoke his first words

6 months: told his doctor, 'I have a left ear infection'

10 months: learned to read

School: didn't go to school; his parents taught him at home; went to high school for one year; graduated and received his high school diploma when he was six

College: went to college to study anthropology; graduated from the college at age ten; *The Guinness Book of Records* lists him as the world's youngest college graduate; appeared on TV chat shows; received a master's degree in biochemistry when he was 14, a master's degree in computer science when he was 18 and a doctorate in chemistry at age 22

Career: started teaching at a college at age seventeen

Other information

2006 and 2008: competed in several TV quiz shows and won over $1,000,000

➤ Go back to page 67.

9.2 Student A

A Write a definition for each word. Start your sentences with '*This is …*' and use an adjective clause.

1 a philanthropist

This is someone who gives money to help people.

2 a course book

______

3 a vegetarian

______

4 a hashtag

______

5 a cell phone

______

6 money

______

B Read your definitions to Student B. Can he/she guess what you are describing?

➤ Go back to page 85.

9.1 Group A

A SPEAK Look at questions 1–3 in Exercise B. What would you do in each situation? Why?

B Think of two more questions. Write them down. Use the second conditional.

1 If you had to choose between having a new cell phone and seeing your favorite band, which would you choose?

2 If you had to choose between a meal for two and an item of clothing, which would you choose?

3 If you could have a weekend break anywhere in the world, where would you go?

4 ______

5 ______

➤ Go back to page 83.

12.2 Group A

Box sets and on-demand viewing are better.

Here are some ideas for your argument. Add some ideas of your own.

- You can watch episodes when you want to and when is convenient for you.
- You will never miss an episode.
- It is easier to find a time to watch an episode or several episodes with other people, which can …

  be a fun social event.

  bring people closer together because of shared interest.

  help people to get to know each other.

➤ Go back to page 115.

11.2 Students A and B

According to psychologists, the first animal you chose is how you like to see yourself. The second animal is how other people see you. And your third choice is what you are really like.

➤ Go back to page 104.

7.1 Student A

A Read the sentences to Student B who will write them down. Be careful to pronounce *a* and *an* using the weak sound /ə/ (schwa). Check Student B's sentences are correct.

1 It was **a** great party.
2 It's **a** really funny movie.
3 It was **an** amazing view.
4 We had **a** lot of fun.
5 It put **a** smile on my face.

B Listen to Student B and write down the sentences he/she says.

C Tell your partner about events or situations that the sentences in Exercise B describe.

A: My sister's 18th birthday was a great party. It was an amazing time and we had a lot of fun. We …
B: It was an amazing view from the top of the Eiffel Tower. I went there last year with …

➤ Go back to page 63.

10.3 Groups

SPEAK Work in groups. Read the fact file and discuss the questions.

Mission to Mars

Distance: When Earth and Mars are closest, the distance between them is 57.6 million kilometers.
Journey time: 6–8 months one-way. Crew will be away from Earth for around two years.
Communication: As the ship moves farther away from Earth, it will take up to 40 minutes to send and receive messages to and from Earth.
Mission: To visit and land on Mars and look for life. Crew will do research and experiments and collect data about the red planet.

1 What will be the biggest challenges for the crew on the mission to Mars?
2 What are the five most important skills and personal qualities crew members will need?
3 What kind of problems might they have to solve on the journey?
4 What will an average day be like on the space ship?

➤ Go back to page 97.

10.2 Student B

A Look at the pictures. Think about how you will answer the questions. Write notes.

1 Can you describe the two pictures?
2 Which of these ways of communicating with other people do you prefer and why?
3 What computer skills and knowledge about the internet does someone need to make video calls?

B DISCUSS Your partner will ask you the questions in Exercise A.

C CHANGE Now ask your partner the questions below.

1 Can you describe the two pictures on page 154?
2 Which of these two ways of managing your money do you prefer and why?
3 What computer skills and knowledge about the internet does someone need to manage an online bank account?

D Can you think of one more question to ask?

➤ Go back to page 95.

12.2 Group B

Traditional weekly TV shows are better.

Here are some ideas for your argument. Add some ideas of your own.

- You look forward to the show more.
- You don't become too obsessed with the show.
- There is no danger of binge-watching, which can …
  be bad for your health or eyesight.
  make your brain too active and cause sleeplessness.
  waste time.

➤ Go back to page 115.

12.3 Groups

Choose one of the products for your advertising campaign.

a

b

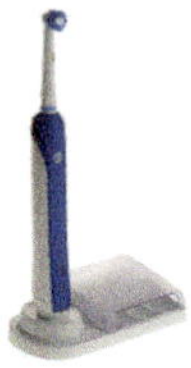

c

➤ Go back to page 117.

10.2 Student A

A Look at the pictures. Think about how you will answer the questions. Write notes.

1 Can you describe the two pictures on page 155?
2 Which of these two ways of managing your money do you prefer and why?
3 What computer skills and knowledge about the internet does someone need to manage an online bank account?

B **DISCUSS** Your partner will ask you the questions in Exercise A.

C **CHANGE** Now ask your partner the following questions.

1 Can you describe the two pictures on page 155?
2 Which of these ways of communicating with other people do you prefer and why?
3 What computer skills and knowledge about the internet does someone need to make video calls?

D Can you think of one more question to ask?

➤ Go back to page 95.

9.2 Student B

A Write a definition for each word. Start your sentences with '*This is …*' and use an adjective clause.

1 a businessman or businesswoman
This is someone who works in business, especially in a top position.
2 a magazine
3 a professor
4 an emoji
5 the internet
6 food

B Read your definitions to Student A. Can he or she guess what you are describing?

➤ Go back to page 85.

12.2 Students A and B

Are you a binge-watcher? Are you addicted to TV?
Take the quiz! Check (✓) the sentences that are true for you. Then read what it means below.

You know you're a binge-watcher and addicted to TV if …

- you have ever said or thought 'Just one more episode'. ☐
- you dream, or daydream, about the show you're currently watching. ☐
- you feel that you know the show's characters as well as your actual friends. ☐
- when the series ends, you feel depressed (for around ten seconds until you start the next one). ☐
- you've stayed up all night, or at least until 3 am, watching episodes of a show. ☐
- the show is your favorite topic of conversation. ☐
- you want other people to watch the show and love it as much as you do. ☐
- watching the show, or even thinking about watching the show, is the best part of your day. ☐

What it means:

1–3 checks: You enjoy watching TV shows. You are not addicted to TV, yet, but you are perhaps an occasional binge-watcher.

4–6 checks: You are addicted to TV and probably a frequent binge-watcher. Be careful this doesn't take over your life.

7–8 checks: You need to get a life!

➤ Go back to page 115.

11.2 Students A and B

Work in pairs. Choose one of the hobbies or activities and give suggestions and advice to improve. Use the phrases in the box.

It's better (not)   It's easy   It's essential   It's good
It's important   It's (not) necessary   It's useful   It's sensible

learn a musical instrument
play a sport
learn a language
keep fit and healthy
live a 'green' lifestyle
keep an animal as a pet
have a job interview
host a party

➤ Go back to page 105.

7.1 Student B

A Listen to Student A and write down the sentences he/she says.

B Read these sentences to Student A, who will write them down. Be careful to pronounce *a* and *an* using the weak sound /ə/ (schwa). Check Student A's sentences are correct.

1 It's **a** great idea.
2 We had **a** fun day.
3 It was **an** amazing time.
4 It was **a** total surprise.
5 He told **a** funny story.

C Tell your partner about events or situations that the sentences in Exercise B describe.

➤ Go back to page 63.

9.1 Group B

A **SPEAK** Look at questions 1–3 in Exercise B. What would you do in each situation? Why?

B Think of two more questions. Write them down. Use the second conditional.

1 If you had to choose between a luxury break for two in your country's capital and the very latest smart television with theater sound, which would you choose?
2 If you had to choose between a well-paid job in a city you don't like and a slightly lower-paid job in a city you like, what would you do?
3 If you won $500, what would you spend it on? What about if you won $5000 or $50,000?
4 ______________________________
5 ______________________________

➤ Go back to page 83.

7.3 Student B

Judit Polgár:
chess Grandmaster

1976: born in Hungary

Education: did not go to school; her parents brought her and her two sisters up as part of an 'educational experiment'; chess was the subject her parents chose

6 years: started playing in international tournaments

9 years: won her first international tournament

15 years: became the youngest person ever to become a chess Grandmaster

Career: was the world's number one female chess player for 20 years; has beaten 11 current or former male world champions

Other information
2012: started the Judit Polgár Chess Foundation; the aim is to introduce children around the world to chess
2014: retired from competitive chess; became head coach of the Hungarian National Men's Chess Team

➤ Go back to page 67.

10.3 Students A and B

Do you have what it takes to work in space? Complete our survey to find out.

Check (✓) the things you do or would like to do in your job.

Follow a detailed schedule ○
Do research and collect data ○
Do experiments and make discoveries ○
Test or work with new technologies ○
Solve problems ○
Repair equipment ○
Work away from home ○
Study the mind or body ○
Do dangerous work ○
Work alone ○
Work in a team ○

Results

1–4 checks: Space is probably not your place.
5–8 checks: You could try a job in the sky.
9+ checks: You'd be great for work on Mars or in the stars.

➤ Go back to page 97.

Ⓦ using survey report language

A Look at the chart. What does it show? Do any of the findings surprise you?

Percentage of population aged 25–34 with a college degree in English-speaking countries in 2015

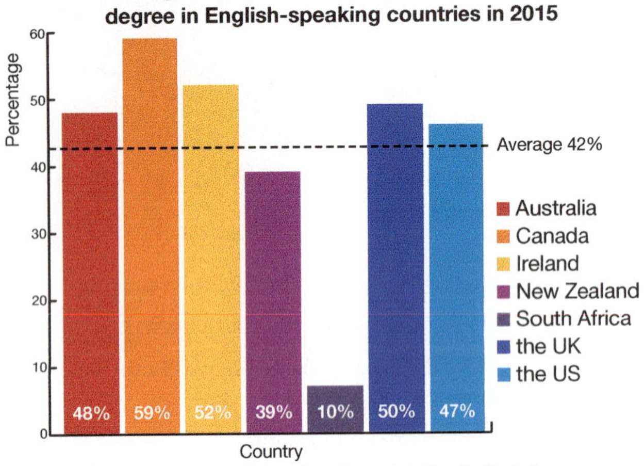

(c) OECD (2018), Population with tertiary education (indicator).

B Complete the survey report with the correct country.

The survey compares the percentage of people aged 25 to 34 with a college degree in English-speaking countries. According to the survey, an average of 42 percent of the population of these countries are graduates. [1]__________ has the highest percentage of graduates at 59 percent. In contrast, [2]__________ has the lowest with just ten percent of the population having a college degree. The number of graduates in [3]__________ is just over 50 percent, while in [4]__________ the figure is just under 50 percent. Similarly, the figure for [5]__________ is 47 percent, while in [6]__________, 39 percent of people aged 25 to 34 are graduates.

C Look at the survey report again and complete the words and phrases in the box.

Using survey report language

We can say what the survey is about with:

- *The survey shows …*
- *The survey* [1]__________ *…*
- *According* [2]__________ *the survey, …*

We can express differences with:

- *By/In comparison, …*
- *By/In* [3]__________*, …*

We can express similarities with:

- [4]__________*, …*
- *Both …*

We can give data and statistics by using:

- *… has the highest percentage of graduates at 59 percent.*
- *… an average of 42 percent of the population …*
- *… has the lowest with just 7 percent …*
- *… the figure for the US is 47 percent …*

Note the different uses of prepositions (*at*, *of*).

D Complete the sentences with the best words or phrases. Use the strategies in the box to help you.

1 As of 2015 the birth rate in the US is just under two children per family. ________________, in Europe it is around 1.5.

2 ________________ the survey, 41 percent of ________________ men and women play sports to keep fit. Thirty percent say they play sports for social reasons.[1]

3 The survey ________________ IQs of brothers and sisters. It ________________ that the oldest generally has the highest IQ.

WRITING

A PREPARE You are going to write a survey report about World Happiness. Read about the report. What areas of life do you think the survey asks questions about?

The World Happiness report is an annual survey. It collects data from over 150 countries to find out which country has the happiest population. The survey asks people to decide how happy they are with different areas of their life.

B PLAN Look at the survey results.

- Decide which of the data you will include.
- Decide how you can compare and contrast the data.
- Use the report in Writing Exercise B to help you.
- Use the information in the *World Happiness* report.
- Use phrases from the Writing skills box.

C WRITE Write about 100–120 words. Check your writing for grammar, vocabulary and spelling.

World Happiness report

Top four countries	score (out of 10)
Norway	7.54
Denmark	7.52
Iceland	7.50
Switzerland	7.50
Bottom four countries	**score**
Syria	3.46
Tanzania	3.35
Burundi	2.91
Central African Republic	2.69

Helliwell, J., Layard, R., & Sachs, J. (2017). World Happiness Report 2017, New York: Sustainable Development Solutions Network.

D DISCUSS Work in groups. Why do you think the countries in the survey are the happiest in the world?

1 Special Eurobarometer 412 "Sport and physical activity". © European Union, 1995-2017

8 Writing — Write a review

W — describing and recommending

A Read the movie review. Is it positive or negative? Underline the words and phrases that tell you this.

La La Land is set in modern-day Los Angeles. It stars Emma Stone and Ryan Gosling. It tells the story of a romance between Mia (played by Emma Stone) and Seb (played by Ryan Gosling). She is an actress and he is a jazz pianist. The movie is a musical, but it is also a classic love story with some wonderful music and singing and some old-fashioned dancing. At the same time, it is exciting, beautiful and heart-breaking. I found myself completely engaged with the story and with the lives of Mia and Seb. The acting was excellent. Emma Stone and Ryan Gosling were perfect as Mia and Seb. If you like musicals, you'll love this movie.

Share Like Comment

Comments:

Stacey99: I agree. Great movie. I wasn't expecting that ending, but it's definitely worth seeing.

BillyTom: I liked the ending. I didn't imagine the story would finish that way. It was a nice twist!

DashaV: This movie is a work of art, full of color and life. A modern-day classic.

Rob78: Not my favorite movie. But to be fair, I don't like musicals!

B Number the topics in the order they are written about in the review.

The movie

___ the plot or story
_1_ where the movie is set (location)
___ writer's opinion of the movie
___ writer's opinion of the actors
___ writer's recommendation
___ movie genre

C Read the comments again. Does each person like or dislike the movie? Underline the words and phrases in the comments that tell you this.

D Cover Exercises A, B and C. Complete the missing words in the phrases from the review and comments.

Describing and recommending

1 *La La Land* is s___ ___ in …
2 It s___ ___ ___ ___ Emma Stone and Ryan Gosling.
3 It tells the s___ ___ ___ ___ of …
4 The m___ ___ ___ ___ is a musical.
5 The a___ ___ ___ ___ ___ was …
6 It's (definitely) w___ ___ ___ ___ seeing.

E Write the missing words to complete the review.

The movie is ___ ___ ___ in Los Angeles in 1961. It ___ ___ ___ ___ ___ the true ___ ___ ___ ___ ___ of the author P.L. Travers and moviemaker Walt Disney. Disney wants to make a movie using one of Traver's books. It ___ ___ ___ ___ ___ Tom Hanks. The ___ ___ ___ ___ ___ ___ is excellent. This movie is definitely ___ ___ ___ ___ ___ seeing.

WRITING

A PREPARE You are going to write review of a movie that you have seen.

B PLAN Take notes for each topic in Writing Exercise B.

C WRITE Use the review in Exercise A and the strategies in the Writing skills box to help you write your review. Write about 100 words.

D REVIEW Work in pairs. Can you find someone in the class who has seen the same movie? Read your partner's review and write a comment. Then work with another pair and add comments to their reviews.

9 Writing ● Write a 'for sale' advertisement

W – describing a product

A Read the advice for writing a 'for sale' advertisement. Complete the advice with the words in the box.

accessories buyer condition details specifications

The key to a great ad

Attention: The title of the advertisement needs to get the [1]___________'s attention. Keep it short and simple. Start with the best or key feature of your item. This could be the price, its [2]___________ or simply that it is a very popular item. If it has a fixed price, use words like 'only' and 'bargain'.

Description: Your advertisement needs a detailed description of the item. If needed, include the [3]___________, such as size, height and width. Include any [4]___________ that it comes with, such as a battery charger. Include pictures to show what condition the item is in.

Action: Encourage the buyer to take action. For example, invite them to contact you with questions or for more [5]___________. Say how you will post the item and offer free postage if possible.

B Look at the advertisements. Do they follow the advice? Find and underline examples of:

- best or key features
- how good the price is
- specification (size or dimensions)
- accessories
- condition
- contacting the seller

digital camera – only $150

The camera is almost new and hardly used. It comes in the original box and with a case, strap and spare battery. See picture. Please contact me if you have any questions.

Pen and ink drawing – auction

This is an original and signed pen and ink drawing by British illustrator William Miller. It shows a mountain scene in Scotland. The dimensions are 35 cm x 18 cm. The work is in good condition with a few minor marks. Please contact me for further information.

Men's sneakers (size 40) – $40

I am selling a pair of sneakers. They are size 40 and are yellow with gray stripes. They are in excellent condition with just a few light marks. I am selling them for the bargain price of $40. Free delivery. If you have any questions, just ask.

C Complete the box with words from the advertisements.

Describing a product

Introducing the item

- *This is …*
- *I am* [1] selling …

Describing its condition, specification and accessories

- *in excellent/good* [2]___________, *almost* [3]___________, *hardly* [4]___________
- *It comes in the original* [5]___________
- *… with (just) a few (light/minor)* [6]___________
- *It comes with …*
- *The dimensions are …*

Contacting the seller

- *Please contact me if you have any (further)* [7]___________.
- *Please contact me for further* [8]___________*/details.*
- *If you have any questions, just* [9]___________.

D Correct the mistakes and rewrite the sentences from online 'for sale' advertisements.

1 The phone comes in the origin box.

____

2 I sell a Sony Bravia 65XE9005 TV.

____

3 The camera is near new and is excellent condition.

____

4 The item in good condition with a few lightly marks.

____

5 Please contact for further informations and details.

____

WRITING

A PLAN You are going to write a 'for sale' advertisement. Choose one of the items in the pictures or choose an item of your own. Invent some details about the condition of the item.

B WRITE Write your advertisement. Use the Writing skills box, the ads and the advice to help you. Write 50–75 words.

C DISCUSS Work in groups. Show your advertisement to your group. Is anyone interested in buying your item?

10 Writing — Write a recommendation

W— making recommendations

A Work in groups. Answer the questions.

1 How many school subjects can you think of in one minute?

2 Which were your favorite and least favorite subjects at school, and why?

3 Were/Are you more interested in science, art, language or humanities (history, geography, etc)?

B Work in pairs. Read Bee's question on an online message board. What recommendation would you make for Bee and why?

Woohaa Answers

Bee, Thailand: Should I buy a laptop or a tablet?
I'm not sure whether to buy a laptop or a tablet. I need a computer for work, but also for entertainment at home and while I'm traveling. What do you think?

C Now read Dylan's answer and underline any ideas you or your partner said in Exercise B. What other advantages and disadvantages of laptops and tablets does Dylan mention?

Best answer
Dylan, US
This is not an easy decision, Bee. If you choose the wrong computer, you might regret it. Before you decide, think about size and weight, performance and price.
Most laptops are bigger and heavier than the average tablet. This is partly because they have a normal keyboard. Size and weight may be a problem if you travel a lot or need to carry your computer to work each day.
When it comes to performance, laptops are usually faster and have a bigger memory than tablets. They are also better for people who need to have several apps or programs open at the same time. On the other hand, the battery in a tablet computer will probably last longer between charges than the one in a laptop.
Of course, your budget is also important. Generally speaking, laptops are more expensive than tablets. If you travel regularly and want to spend less money, I'd recommend a tablet. If you want better performance and a normal keyboard, I'd suggest buying a laptop.
I think you should do some more research online. You could also talk to someone in a computer store and ask for their opinion. Good luck!

D Read the information in the box. Then find and underline four examples of the structures in the box in Dylan's answer.

Making recommendations

You can tell people what you think they should do using the following language:

- *I think you should* + base form
- *You could* + base form
- *I'd suggest* + noun **or** verb + *-ing* **or** *you* + base form
- *I'd recommend* + noun **or** verb-*ing* **or** *you* + base form

E There is one mistake in each recommendation. Correct the mistakes.

1 I think you should getting a new phone rather than a used one.

____

2 I'd recommend you checking a used phone carefully before you buy it.

____

3 You could reading more about different brands online.

____

4 I'd suggest to buy a used phone because you'll get better performance for your money.

____

F Work in pairs. Imagine a friend has asked you the following questions. What would you recommend and why? Compare your ideas.

1 Should I travel for six months or get a job right away when I finish college?

2 What brand of computer do you think I should I buy?

3 Should I study science or language?

WRITING

A WRITE Read Corey's question on the *Woohaa Answers* website. Write a reply of at least 100 words comparing the two options and making recommendations.

Woohaa Answers

Corey, Germany: Should I buy a new or used phone?
Should I buy a new cell phone or a used one? I don't have a lot of money to spend on it, but I'd like the best one I can afford. What do you think?

B REVIEW Work in groups. Read your group's recommendations. In what ways are they similar or different to yours?

11 Writing

Write an email giving suggestions and advice

W– making suggestions and giving advice

A Look at the places in the pictures. Where do you think they are? Read the emails quickly and match them with the pictures. Were your ideas correct?

1

2

3

a
To: Sam
Subject: RE: Any advice?

You really must visit the Joshua Tree National Park when you're in California. It isn't far from Los Angeles and it's really easy to get to by car. It's named after the famous Joshua trees that are found there. It's an amazing desert landscape with huge rocks and boulders everywhere. If I were you, I'd spend at least two days there. You can camp there, but it's a good idea to book in advance.

b
To: Carlos
Subject: RE: Vietnam tips

In Vietnam, Halong Bay is a must. There are thousands of different-sized islands and rock formations coming out of the ocean. It really is an incredible place. According to legend, the bay was formed when an angry dragon destroyed a mountain with its tail. It isn't too far from Hanoi. I'd recommend taking an organized tour from there.

c
To: Teresa
Subject: RE: Where to go

If you're in northern England, you really should visit the island of Lindisfarne. It's about a mile from the mainland and you can drive across to it when the tide is out. But when the tide comes in, it becomes a true island. It's a magical place with some beautiful beaches. I suggest you head to the north part of the island to get away from the crowds of people. Make sure you check the times of the tides so you know when it's safe to cross.

B Read again and complete the table.

	a	b	c
Name of place			
Location			
Key features			
How to travel there			

C Complete the box with words from the emails.

Making suggestions and giving advice

When/If you're in …
I suggest you …
I'd [1] ____________ + verb + *-ing …*
You (really) [2] ____________ */ ought to / must …*
If I [3] ____________ *you, I* [4] ____________ *…*
… is a must.
Make [5] ____________ *you …*
It's a good [6] ____________ *to …*

D Write the words in the correct order to make sentences.

1 It's / to / a / book the train in advance / idea / good
2 I / in April or May / suggest / go / you
3 I'd / at least two or three days / staying / recommend
4 If / in Krakow, / you're / the Wieliczka Salt Mine / visit / really / you / should
5 When / in Oxford, / you're / make / you / sure / the Natural History Museum / visit
6 If / I'd / you, / were / I / for a few days / rent a car

WRITING

A PLAN Imagine a friend is visiting your country or a country you know. You are going to write a short email (50–100 words) to make some suggestions and to give some advice about a place to visit.

B WRITE Use the Writing skills box and include information about:

- where it is
- how to get there
- the main features of the place

C REVIEW Work in groups. Read each other's emails. Which place would you most like to visit?

12 Writing

Write a story

W writing a story

A Work in pairs. Read the news story then close your books and retell the story to your partner. What do you think of Brett Sanders's actions?

Texan driver paid speeding ticket with over 22,000 pennies.

Brett Sanders was driving at 39 mph in a 30 mph zone when he was stopped by police and was given a $212 fine.

Sanders said the fine was too much and that he wanted to make some kind of complaint. So, he ordered over $212 in pennies from the bank and put them into two large buckets. He then went to the payment office and poured the 22,000 coins onto the counter. When he had finished this, he immediately walked out of the building. A friend filmed him while he was doing this. He told reporters that after he had done it, he 'felt great'.

According to the payment office, Sanders had actually overpaid by $7.81. They called him to offer a refund, but Sanders was happy to let them keep the change.

Many people have said Sanders's actions were wrong. At the same time, other people think it was a good way to make a point. What do you think?

B Look at the box. Find and underline more examples of the three tenses in the news story.

Writing a story

Tenses

When we tell a story, we usually use three main tenses.

We use the simple past for the main events in the story.

- *So, he ordered over $212 in pennies from the bank and put them into two large buckets.*

We use the past progressive for background activities or situations that were in progress when the main events happened.

- *Brett Sanders was driving at 39 mph in a 30 mph zone when he was stopped by police and was given a $212 fine.*

We use the past perfect for events that happened before one of the main events or that happened before the time of the story.

- *When he had finished this, he immediately walked out of the building.*

Sequence words

We use sequence words to connect the events and make the sequence clear.

- *Brett Sanders was driving at 39 mph in a 30 mph zone when he was stopped by police ...*
- *So, he ordered over $212 in pennies from the bank ...*
- *He then went to the payment office and poured the 22,000 coins onto the counter. When he had finished this, he immediately walked out of the building.*
- *A friend filmed him while he was doing this. He told reporters that after he had done it, he 'felt great'.*

C Choose the correct words to complete the news story.

A surfer [1]***was rescued / had been rescued*** yesterday [2]***while / after*** he [3]***was spending / had spent*** 32 hours at sea. It [4]***got / was getting*** dark [5]***when / then*** the helicopter rescue team [6]***spotted / were spotting*** him 13 miles off the coast of Scotland. He [7]***was / had been*** exhausted and thirsty, but he survived as he [8]***wore / was wearing*** a wetsuit and [9]***was / had been*** still on his surfboard.

WRITING

A PREPARE Look at the pictures and imagine what the story is. You are going to write a short story using all the pictures. Use this as you first sentence:

A man was arrested yesterday for driving a children's electric car.

B PLAN Takes notes and think about the tenses and the sequence words you need to use.

C WRITE Write the story (130–150 words). Check what you have written and make any necessary changes.

D REVIEW Work in groups. Read some of your classmates' stories. How similar are your stories?

Audio scripts

UNIT 7

Lesson 7.3, Listening, Exercise C

7.4 **S = Shauna**

S: Welcome to *Great Minds*. I'm Shauna Andrews, and today we're talking about William James Sidis. You have possibly never heard of him. But he is perhaps one of the most intelligent people who ever lived. He had an IQ of between 250 and 300.

He was born in the United States in 1898, and grew up in New York. His parents, who were originally from Ukraine, were doctors and were both highly intelligent.

They wanted to give their son the best possible chance in life. So, his mother gave up her job and taught him at home. He didn't go to school. And they brought him up to have a 'love of knowledge'.

As a result, Sidis was reading and writing at 18 months, and enjoyed reading the *New York Times* newspaper. He wrote several books and newspaper articles before he was four and, by the time he was eight, he spoke seven languages. He also made up his own language, which he called 'Vendergood'. At 11, he went to college to study math – to Harvard University, actually. And in fact, he had previously given a math lecture there when he was nine. Sidis became front page news and news reporters followed him everywhere at the college. He became known as a child prodigy all over the country.

Sidis graduated from Harvard University with a degree in mathematics at age 16. He then joined Rice University as a teacher of math. However, he found teaching difficult, especially because of his age. After only eight months, he left Rice University and went back to Harvard, this time to study law.

While studying law, he became more and more interested in the political and social issues of the day. And as a result, he dropped out of the university before he finished his degree. This was a big turning point in his life. Soon after, in 1918, he was arrested while he was taking part in an anti-war demonstration. He received an 18-month prison sentence. However, he didn't go to prison and instead he spent a year in a hospital. It was actually the hospital where his parents worked.

After this, Sidis tried to stay out of the public eye. He moved from city to city around America and he had a number of simple low-paid jobs. He became more and more lonely and finally, he had a falling out with his parents and lost contact with them. The newspapers printed stories about how the child prodigy had failed as an adult.

After his death in 1944, many people questioned his high IQ and many of his other childhood achievements. Despite this, Sidis has been the subject of a number of books and academic studies and he is still one of the world's greatest child prodigies.

UNIT 8

Lesson 8.1, Listening, Exercise C

8.2 **L = Lizzie S = Suzy**

L: Welcome to *Music matters* with me, Lizzie Reid. Our taste in music says a lot about who we are. But why do we have different tastes in music? To answer this question, we are joined by Professor Suzy Harrison, an expert in the psychology of music. Welcome, Suzy.

S: Hello, thank you.

L: So, why do some people, say, prefer rock music or blues or jazz, while other people prefer pop or rap music?

S: Well, there are three main points which might explain our taste in music. The first is the music we grew up with. We don't choose this music ourselves, of course. But as a child, the music that we hear at home is familiar and comforting. Later in life, these same sounds bring back these feelings and this gives us pleasure. So, when we start to discover music by ourselves, it is influenced by what we listened to when we were growing up.

L: So, you're saying our first musical influence is our parents and our brothers and sisters?

S: Yes, that's right – particularly, our older brothers and sisters. Secondly, music brings people together. It creates an atmosphere and mood that people can share. So the second point is that we listen to certain types of music to help us form or join social groups. We want to be with people similar to ourselves. In contrast, for other people, musical taste is a way to make themselves different from other people. It's a way to be an individual. If you listen to music that others don't like, people will see you differently.

L: Yes, and I suppose it's true that we are generally attracted to people with similar music tastes to our own.

S: Yes, that's generally the case. And the third point is about how we feel when we listen to the music. Music can help to create a mood! For example, when you want to study, you might listen to something in the background, something without words – classical music, for example. And when you're preparing for a night out, you might want to energize yourself and play something loud and full of energy – maybe some rock or pop or reggae music. At other times, you might play the same sad song over and over again. Because of the internet, finding music is very quick and easy for our different moods. Interestingly, studies have shown that because of this easy access to different kinds of music, people today like a much wider range of music styles compared to previous generations.

L: I see. So, our individual taste in music is a combination of three things: the music we grew up with, the need to fit in with other people and finally, to match our different moods?

S: Yes, that's right. Of course, one thing may be stronger than the others. But, yes, over time it is most likely a combination of these things which influence our music choices.

L: Very interesting, Professor Harrison. Thank you for speaking to us today.

S: You're welcome.

Lesson 8.3, Listening, Exercise C

8.7

A: … Well, I'd say the main difference between movies and books is how they tell the story and how we connect with it.

B: Yes, I agree. Books allow the reader to use their imagination. We can visualize the story and the people and the places in our own way. With movies, on the other hand, we see what the director and the actors want us to see. There's much less possibility for us to use our own imagination.

A: I agree. And another important difference is that with books, the story generally moves more slowly and goes into more detail. With a movie, though, the whole story needs to start and finish in 90 minutes. So, in a book, we have more time to get to know the characters and to understand them. I think this makes the experience more personal and engaging.

B: Well, yes, I see what you mean – a book can be more engaging, but at the same time, a movie can be much more exciting and gripping than a book. It can use sounds and images and dialogue all at the same time. We use our different senses. And for many people, this is more entertaining than reading a book. Music can also make the movie more interesting and memorable.

A: That's true. I think another important difference is that with a book, the chapters provide natural breaks in the story. This gives us time to think about what we have read. A movie doesn't give us this opportunity.

B: Yeah, and also, of course, watching a movie is usually a social experience. We generally watch a movie with other people and then talk about it and share our opinions. But reading a book is more individual and personal. I think that's a really important difference.

A: Yes, I agree that reading is a less sociable activity. Although, book clubs are very popular these days. I guess that's a similar social experience.

B: And one more thing is that people usually say that the book is better than the movie. Compared to the book, people usually say they are disappointed by the movie – especially if they have read the book first. However, I think in many cases people actually prefer the movie.

A: Interesting. That's something that we can …

Lesson 8.3, Listening, Exercise E

8.8

1 Books allow the reader to use their imagination. With movies, on the other hand, we see what the director and the actors want us to see.

2 With books, the story generally moves more slowly. With a movie, though, the whole story needs to start and finish in 90 minutes.

3 We generally watch a movie with other people … But reading a book is more individual and personal.

4 Reading is a less sociable activity. Although, book clubs are very popular these days.

5 People usually say they are disappointed by the movie. However, in many cases people actually prefer the movie.

Lesson 8.3, Vocabulary, Exercise B

8.9

1 It was totally engaging and the acting was amazing.

2 I was, well, a little bored by the end. It isn't very memorable, I'm afraid.

3 You won't be disappointed. The singing was incredible.

4 It's really gripping. And it's very moving and sad, too.

UNIT 9

Lesson 9.2, Listening, Exercise B

9.3

Today's lecture is about philanthropy. Philanthropy, as you know, is the act of giving away a large amount of money which is used to benefit society.

There are many famous and not so famous people who have given away large amounts of money. Two of the 20th century's most famous philanthropists are John D. Rockefeller and Andrew Carnegie. Rockefeller of course made his money from oil and Carnegie from the steel industry. Rockefeller gave away about $540 million before his death in 1937, and Carnegie gave away about $350 million. This was about 90 percent of his wealth. And today there are many celebrities who have given money to charity. For example, the TV personality Oprah Winfrey has so far given away around half a billion dollars.

But perhaps today's most well-known philanthropists are Bill Gates and his wife Melinda, and Warren Buffett. Their main aim is to improve global health and to end poverty. And between them, they have already given away tens of billions of dollars. In 2010, they also created the Giving Pledge. The Giving Pledge asks …

Lesson 9.2, Listening, Exercise D

9.4

But perhaps today's most well-known philanthropists are Bill Gates and his wife Melinda, and Warren Buffett. Their main aim is to improve global health and to end poverty. And between them, they have already given away tens of billions of dollars. In 2010, they also created the Giving Pledge. The Giving Pledge asks the world's richest people to give away at least half of their wealth in their lifetime. In its first ten years, many people agreed to this, including Facebook's Mark Zuckerberg, Virgin boss Richard Branson and Ann Gloag, who started the international transportation group Stagecoach.

However, not everyone agrees that the Giving Pledge is a good thing, and some people have decided not to join. So, let's now look at five modern-day philanthropists that you may or may not have heard of.

First, Carlos Slim. Slim is a Mexican businessman and is one of the world's richest men. He made his money in telecommunications and is worth around $80 billion. He has so far given away about $8 billion. However, he has not joined the Giving Pledge because he disagrees with the approach of Bill Gates and Warren Buffet. Instead, he believes that education and jobs are the best way to end poverty.

Next, we have Sara Blakely, an American businesswoman. She recently became the world's youngest self-made female billionaire, and she was also the first woman to join the Giving Pledge. Her philanthropy focuses mainly on women's and girls' education and career possibilities. She believes that if there are more women in powerful positions, this will make the world a better place.

Li Ka-shing is a Hong Kong businessman and has promised to give away one third of his $30 billion fortune. His aim is to promote education and health, but mainly in China. He has not joined the Giving Pledge. This is because he wishes to keep control of how and when he gives his money away.

Billionaire Meg Whitman was the president of eBay for ten years. She has said that she would refuse if she was invited to join the Giving Pledge. Instead, she has her own charity that focuses on the environment and education.

And finally, Azim Premji. Premji is one of India's richest people. He has joined the Giving Pledge and has already given away one quarter of his wealth. Premji's aim is to improve Indian school education and he has also set up a university which promotes educational thinking.

So, what do you think? Is the Giving Pledge a good thing? And what about philanthropy in general? What are the pros and the cons of this …

UNIT 10

Lesson 10.1, Listening, Exercise A

10.1

1: I travel and fly a lot for work, and this device means my bag is a lot lighter than it used to be. I can honestly say it's the best gadget I've ever bought. Before I got it, I always used to carry three or four heavy novels with me, but now I can fit hundreds into my coat pocket. I bought the cheapest one, but the battery lasts for a long time and it has a dictionary. You can check words so much more quickly than in a paper dictionary. You just touch the word you don't know and it shows you the meaning.

2: This is definitely the most useful piece of technology I own. I don't enjoy driving in new cities or foreign countries, but I can find my way so much more easily than in the past thanks to this smart device. Obviously, it was more expensive than an old-fashioned paper map, but I don't regret buying it. My wife and I don't argue about which way to go anymore! It's very reliable – it never makes mistakes and even tells you when there is traffic or a speed camera.

3: This has to be the greatest invention of the 21st century! I take it everywhere with me and it is just the right size to fit in my bag. They are getting cheaper and cheaper – mine cost less than a lot of phones do these days. I don't have many apps on it, and most of the time, I just use it to go online or watch videos – the screen is so much bigger than on my phone. The best thing about it is that it starts so quickly. It's much faster and more convenient than my old laptop. The worst thing about it is that I now spend even more time online!

4: Every Saturday morning, I go to the city park and meet other … uh … fans. We spend a lot of time talking about our favorite 'toys', as my girlfriend calls them, and arguing about which is the best, or which turns the most quickly, or a thousand other things! And of course we fly and race them. Mine is a little heavier than some of them because it has a camera, but I can take pictures and videos from the air. And of course, they are not just for fun – they have many possible uses. You know, delivering packages, helping the police, taking pictures for scientific research and so on.

UNIT 11

Lesson 11.1, Listening, Exercise B

11.3 **P = Presenter M = Mike**

P: Welcome to this week's edition of the *Travel Show*. Today, we are joined by travel writer Mike Harold. A year ago, Mike decided to visit the Seven Natural Wonders of the World. Last week, he finally achieved his goal. Mike, tell us a little about the seven natural wonders.

M: Well, the Seven Natural Wonders of the World was the idea of the Seven Natural Wonders organization. The organization was created to promote and to protect the natural wonders of the world. Not just these seven, but many others as well.

P: So, how did they choose the seven places?

M: The decision was based on three main things. The places were chosen according to how unique the place is, how important it is and, finally, its pure natural beauty.

P: And why did you decide to visit them?

M: Well, I've always loved traveling and I like a challenge! As a travel writer, I thought this was an interesting thing to do professionally.

P: OK, so, what are the seven natural wonders?

M: First, I visited the Great Barrier Reef. The reef is 2600 km long and is located off the northeastern coast of Australia. It's made of over 400 different kinds of coral and is the largest and most colorful coral reef in the world. It really was amazing.

After that, I went to the Grand Canyon, in the US. It was chosen as a natural wonder because of its enormous size and incredible scenery. The canyon was created by the Colorado River, which you can see at the very bottom. It's the most popular of the seven natural wonders and is visited by over five million people a year.

The next place was the most difficult to get to, as it's located in the Himalayan mountain range.

P: Ohh, this has to be Mount Everest!

M: Yes, the highest place on Earth. I didn't go to the top, but I went to the base camp, which is at about 5000 meters. The views were unbelievable.

P: I can imagine. And where did you go next?

M: My fourth natural wonder was Victoria Falls. This, of course, is the famous waterfall on the Zambezi River in southern Africa. It is actually on the border of two countries, Zambia and Zimbabwe. The waterfall is almost two kilometers wide and over 100 meters high. It really was an incredible sight.

For numbers five and six, I traveled to Central and South America. The first is perhaps the least well known. It's the Paricutin volcano in Mexico.

P: Yes, I must admit, I've never heard of this.

M: Well, it was only formed in 1943, so it's fairly new! It was also the first time modern science saw the creation of a volcano – and that's why it's a natural wonder. I was able to climb the volcano and walk around the crater and look inside. I then went to South America to see a more familiar 'wonder' – the bay and natural harbor of Rio de Janeiro in Brazil. The bay includes several islands and is surrounded by beautiful beaches and spectacular mountains with some great views.

P: And I understand for the final natural wonder, you had some good luck.

M: Yes, I did. The final natural wonder I saw was the northern lights, or aurora borealis. I went to Iceland to see them. You can only see them at certain times of the year. And yes, I was very lucky. It really was amazing. And the perfect way to finish my challenge.

P: That sounds amazing! Thanks for sharing your journey with us.

UNIT 12

Lesson 12.3, Listening, Exercise C

12.4 **K = Kerry A = Alex**

K: Hi, Alex, over here!

A: Hey, Kerry, long time no see! Isn't this amazing?!

K: What's going on? It's so busy!

A: YES! She did it.

K: Did what? What is this?

A: Well, it's an ad campaign for sneakers. If you run past the ad, past the billboard, … if you run fast enough, you win a pair of sneakers. It's smart, isn't it?

K: Oh, yeah. That's really cool. And yes, a really smart idea. What brand is it for? I can't see a logo or anything.

A: It's for Reebok, I think. Yes, look, there's the Reebok logo.

K: And what's 'fast enough'? Does it say how fast you have to run?

A: I'm not sure, but everyone seems to be going pretty quickly. Look, watch this guy … Go! Go! … Oh, no. He didn't do it.

K: You should try it, Alex. Go on. Win yourself some new sneakers. You're a fast runner, aren't you?

A: Actually, I'm not so sure I am, to be honest. I think I'll just watch.

K: We were talking about advertising in a class at the university last week. Have you seen that one for vacuum cleaners? That's another smart one.

A: I'm not sure. What is it?

K: Well, they made a video of cars going through a tunnel. They then added a billboard to the background which showed a huge vacuum cleaner so that it looked like the cars were sucked into the vacuum cleaner.

A: Oh, I think I have seen that, actually.

K: And when they put the video online, people didn't know if it was real or just a video. It created a lot of interest and discussion. It was a very successful ad.

A: Oh, I see. I thought it was a real billboard.

K: No, it's just a video. They did it because they didn't have enough money for an actual billboard campaign.

A: Oh, that's really smart. Really original. And simple.

K: Yes, that's what we were talking about in the class last week – what makes a good ad. And it's exactly that in my opinion – something simple and original.

A: Yeah, and something with a clear message, something you can connect with. And a catchy slogan you can easily remember, you know, like McDonald's 'I'm lovin' it'.

K: Yeah, but I think the most important thing is that it catches your eye and gets your attention in the first place. Like this Reebok one.

A: Yeah, I agree. You know what, I think I might try it. Should I?

K: Yes, go for it. You can do it. Alex, Alex, Alex …

Macmillan Education Limited
4 Crinan Street
London N1 9XW

Companies and representatives throughout the world

American Language Hub Level 2B Student's Book ISBN 978-1-380-04709-0
American Language Hub Level 2B Student's Book with Student's App
ISBN 978-1-380-04703-8

Written by Daniel Brayshaw and Jon Hird
With thanks to Edward Price and Carol Goodwright for additional authoring and to Signature Manuscripts for the Grammar Hub pages.

First published 2020

Designed by emc design ltd
Illustrated by Peter Lubach, Rasmus Juul, Rose Frith represented by Lemonade Illustration
Cover design by Restless
Cover image by Getty Images/Linghe Zhao
Picture research by Emily Taylor and Victoria Gaunt
Café Hub videos produced by Creative Listening
Café Hub video scripts written by James and Luke Vyner

Authors' acknowledgements

Daniel Brayshaw would like to thank the whole team for their invaluable support. Also, a special thanks to Sue Kay and Vaughan Jones for all their advice and guidance, and to my wife, Lucyna Brayshaw, for everything. Last but not least to Flash, our dog, for insisting I take regular breaks from the desk. Good boy.

Jon Hird would like to thank the Macmillan Education Editorial team for their input, ideas and hard work in shaping the content of the book.

The authors and publishers would like to thank the following for permission to reproduce their photographs:

Alamy pXIX(2-band), AF archive p76(5), Claudio Baldini p70(c), Axel Bueckert p69(3), the box studio pXXIII(c), Cultura Creative (RF) p82, John Davidson Photos pXXI(6), Stephen Dorey/Bygone Images pXXVIII(bcl), Gioia Emidi pXXI(10.1-6), Jürgen Fälchle p96, Photo Stock/National Geographic Creative p71, Givaga p69(7), Ted Horowitz pXX(5), itdarbs pXXXI, Natallia Khlapushyna p69(8), Metta image p69(2), Minden Pictures p104(t), Losevsky Pavel pXIX(1-band), Photo 12 p76(6), robertharding pp102(7), XX(7), Unknown p84(tr), Alex Witt p101; **Anastassia Elias** p74(d); **Bananastock** p69 (background); **Banksy**, London, 2004 p75(d); **Bridgeman Images** Little Dancer, Aged 14, viewed from the back (polychrome bronze, satin ribbon & wood) (see also 100777), Degas, Edgar (1834-1917)/ Private Collection/Photo © Christie's Images p75(a), Guitar on a Chair (oil on canvas), Gris, Juan (1887-1927)/Private Collection/Photo © BEBA/AISA pXX(4); Mona Lisa, c.1503-6 (oil on panel), Vinci, Leonardo da (1452-1519) / Louvre, Paris, France pXX(3); **Corbis** pp102(3); **Getty Images** pp70(a,b), XXI(1), alexxl66 pXXVIII(bl), Daniel Allan p99(background), Sally Anscombe pp61, Archive Photos p66(cr), ARB p66(tr), Raul Arboleda p66(cl), jez_bennett p105(e), Bettmann p84(l), pXX(6), Tyler Boley p111, bopav p89(scarf), Hervé Bois/EyeEm p81, Peter Cade p114(t), iStockphoto/caimacanul p89(jeans), Colin Carter Photography p105(b), Sandra Clegg p79(b), EyeEm/Pinghung Chen p69(c), L. Cohen/WireImage pXXII(t), The Print Collector/Print Collector pXX(1), Jim Cumming p105(d), Caiaimage/ Robert Daly pXXV(l), DeAgostini p102(5), iStockphoto/demidoffaleks p89(jacket), David Doubilet p102(6), filadendron pXX(a), Antonio de Moraes Barros Filho P62(d), www.galerie-ef.de p78(b), Katherine Gaines pXXI(4), Vincent van Gogh p75(c), Bill Greenblatt/ AFP p66(b), grinvalds p112, Izabela Habur pp65, iStockphoto Thinkstock Images/ halfbinz pXXI(7), istockphoto/StHelena p77, Hero Images pp72(background), Blend Images/Ronnie Kaufman/Larry Hirshowitz pXX(e), Stephan Hoeck pXXIV(r), Andrew Howe p89(background), icreative p89(shirt), Emma Innocenti p114(b), iStockphoto Thinkstock Images/johny007pan p118(background), Mark Keelan pXXX(l), Dorling Kindersley p89(skirt), Thomas Koidhis p102(1), Nicole Kucera p102(4), Liquidlibrary p86(t), simonlong pXXI(2), Lumina Images p89(bl), Dawid Markiewicz p62(f), Scott Masterton pXXX(m), Maurusone p98(b), Ian McKinnell p113, Sabrina Bekeschus Monteiro/EyeEm p108(background), Naumoid p147(6), Steve De Neef p105(f), Michael Ochs Archives p62(b), iStockphoto/Thinkstock Images/Edu_Oliveros p69(4), James O'Neil pXXX(r), PeopleImages p64, Prasit photo p93, oneinchpunch p83, Rudy Orozco P8(croissants), Pobytov p109(background), Getty/PhotoDisc pp98(bcr), XXVIII(cml), Martin Poole pXX(c), Prasit photo pXXIX, Jack Reynolds p105(a), RG-vc pXXVIII(cr), Nicholas Roberts/AFP p84(br), Paul Rojas p102(2), Kirill Rudenko pXXV(r), iStockphoto/scanrail pXXVIII(cmr), Daniel Schoenen /LOOK-foto pp62(b), 63(b), Davide Seddio pXXI(2), shayes17 p109(b), Ariel Skelley pXXIII(bl), skynesher p91, spooh pXXI(5), Daniel Smith pXX(f), by sonmez p118(b), SolStock p92, kaisphoto p89(t-shirt), George Stroud p66(tr), studiocasper pXXVIII(cl), Santi Sukarnjanaprai p103, Superstock pXX(2), Tarzhanova p89(dress), Tetra Images pp95, XX(b), Thinkstock Images/Jupiterimages pXX(8), Lise Ulrich Fine Art Photography p105(c), Universal History Archive/UIG p75(b), Universal Images Group pp62(a), Wavebreakmedia pXXI(10.1-2), Westend61 ppXXI(10.1-5), Barry Willis pXXIII(br), iStockphoto/Thinkstock Images/Steven Wynn p66(tl), Carol Yepes pXX(d); **Mayer** McCann Erickson Slovakia p116(tr,cr,br); **Nature Picture Library** Ingo Arndt p104(b); **Rex/Shutterstock** pXXVII, David Boily p86(b), Universal History Archive p76(2), Rob Latour/Variety p84(br), IMAS/JENNIFER LAVERS HANDOUT/EPA p106(t,b), Lucasfilm/Bad Robot/Walt Disney Studios/Kobal p76(1), Peter Schneider/Epa pXXV(tr); **Robin Nilssen**, Boon Photography. Creative Agency: Animal p116(tl,cl,bl); **Shutterstock**/Cubolabo p69(1), Yulia Glam p62(e); **Solent News & Photo Agency** Stanislav Aristov p74(c); **STOCKBYTE** pXXI(3); **Stockphoto** Bulgac pXXIII(b); **Scott Wade** p74(b); **Max Zorn** p74(a); **123RF** Elnur Amikishiyev p62(c), Tyler Olson pXXI(10.1-4), Baiba Opule p69(5), Andriy Popov pXXI(10.1-1), pXXIV(l), Irina Roibu p69(6), Stockfotocz pXXI(10.1-3).

Commissioned photographs in the Café Hubs by Creative Listening.

The authors and publishers are grateful for permission to reprint the following copyright material:

p106 Eriksen M, Lebreton LCM, Carson HS, Thiel M, Moore CJ, Borerro JC, et al. (2014) Plastic Pollution in the World's Oceans: More than 5 Trillion Plastic Pieces Weighing over 250,000 Tons Afloat at Sea. PLoS ONE 9(12): e111913. https://doi.org/10.1371/journal.pone.0111913; p106 Extract from '38 million pieces of plastic waste found on uninhabited South Pacific island' by Elle Hunt. Originally published in The Guardian, 15 May 2017. © Copyright Guardian News & Media Ltd 2018. Reprinted with permission of The Guardian; p107 Extract from 'Marine Conservation Society' © Marine Conservation Society (MCS) 2017. Reprinted with permission of Marine Conservation Society; p106 Significant anthropogenic debris on remote island, Jennifer L. Lavers, Alexander L. Bond. Proceedings of the National Academy of Sciences Jun 2017, 114 (23) 6052-6055; DOI: 10.1073/pnas.1619818114; p112 Extract from 'Here is Facebook's guide to fake news' by Aatif Sulleyman. Originally published in The Independent, 9 May 2017. © Independent Digital News and Media Ltd 2017. Reprinted with permission of The Independent; p114 Extract from 'How binge-watching has changed TV forever' by Sarah Rainey. Originally published in The Telegraph, 22 January 2015. © Telegraph Media Group Limited 2015. Reprinted with permission of The Telegraph; pXXVI Helliwell, J., Layard, R., & Sachs, J. (2017). World Happiness Report 2017, New York: Sustainable Development Solutions Network.

Printed and bound in Uruguay

2023

6